Getting Beyond What Is

Getting Beyond What Is

TAKING BACK YOUR LIFE

Michael Nulty

Print ISBN-13: 978-1-5272-1709-6

Designer: Euan Monaghan
Editor: Sarah Abel

Contents

I dedicate this book to my mother
who taught me that when you have the will
you will find the way.

Acknowledgments

To my loving partner, Joe who's been by my side through the brightest and darkest of times, always loving and supporting me in everything I do.

They say your family are the friends you choose but my friends are the family I have. Thank you Gerry, Martin, Sheamus and my amazing sister, Maria for all of your love, support and kindness.

Thank you Louise Hay for your wisdom. You have helped me heal my life many times over. Sadly, Louise transitioned in August of this year.

Abraham-Hicks's teachings have taken me through the darkest of my days. Thank you Esther and Jerry for your wonderful work. You can find out more about the teachings of Abraham-Hicks at www.abraham-hicks.com.

About the Author

Three years ago Michael's life look pretty great. He was successful, travelled around the world, had lots of money, a loving partner, family and friends. It seemed like a perfect life. However, Michael felt that there was something missing, he believed that there was something more, something greater beyond the life he was living. So, with a mind full of possibilities and dreams, he embarked on a new journey at the age of forty-nine, to explore and embrace life in a very different way. He didn't realize it at the time but, before he would ever know if there was something more, he would lose everything and fight a battle for his own life.

Beginning a life of uncertainty awakened dormant unconscious past experiences and old limiting beliefs, changing what he thought was possible into struggles and his dreams of something greater into nightmares. He became imprisoned by the mind that once helped him change his life to get beyond his childhood years of being bullied, years of depression as a teenager and young adult, suicide attempts and business losses. Now, unsure of who he was and uncertain of this new life he was creating, he lost himself and fell into a state of deep depression.

Getting Beyond What Is

Michael's story is remarkable, because in the midst of despair he found hope and a connection that changed his entire perspective and relationship with life. He found a new appreciation and awareness for all of his life, past and present that life was happening through him not in spite of him. In *Getting Beyond What Is: Taking back your life*, Michael shares what he wished he'd known when his whole world collapsed and he went through his own very dark times – how he was able to get beyond his depression and struggles to take back his life by making choices that invited new possibilities – new ways of thinking, feeling, behaving and living life in a different and better way.

While you continue to allow hardships past and present impact your life you become stuck in a cycle of brokenness, and a feeling of hopelessness, unable to fully allow or accept new ways of doing anything to make your life better. A greater life can only begin when you take the time to change your own self first. So, come on a journey with Michael and let him help bring light and hope again into your life.

Testimonials

Michael quickly gained wide-spread recognition when he began sharing his story across social media. Over the past year he has inspired, empowered and helped thousands of people around the world to get through difficult life events and resist the temptation to give up on their dreams and finding their life of purpose, love and happiness. Here's what some of his fans have to say:

"Whenever I'm struggling or feeling low, your quotes save me. They remind me that it's okay and inspire me on how to take control and move forward" – Mental Health Martha, USA

Your words seem to be exactly what I need to hear/see on that day. You help keep me on track to self-love, self-compassion and healing" – Carrie Fitzroy, Canada

"No one is fighting the same battle as me – we all have unique stories and experiences. But you help me smile and give me hope on days I think I may never smile again" – Merryn Coutts, Australia

Getting Beyond What Is

"Consistently comforting and thought producing posts. Helping and healing hearts and minds with your daily dose of care. Thank you my friend" John Moore, Northern Ireland

"Sometimes when my emptiness is fighting intrusive damaging thoughts, your words fall upon my heart and the pain dulls" – Julie Worthington, United Kingdon

"Mental illness always finds a way to creep in, so posts like yours always help. Stable or unstable we all need positive reinforcement and when it comes from someone who has gone through it, it means even more" – Jake Waldron, USA

"You are gifted with the ability to say the right thing at right time. Your words keep me hanging in for my breakthrough" – Stephanie Smith, Australia

"I don't know if it's by coincidence or design but Michael's posts always mirror what's going on with my thoughts. Looking forward to more" – Pat Snow, USA

CHAPTER ONE

Making Choices

I was twenty-three when I attempted suicide for the first time. It was the hardest and very darkest of times. A time that had long passed and a period of my life that I never thought I would face again. As my world, the life I had created unravelled and dissolved into pieces around me, I was there in that dark place again. I had gone so far forward only to find myself relapsing into an all too familiar place twenty-seven years later.

I believed I was on the right path, doing the right things. I thought I understood it all. I had spent over twenty years learning, expanding my knowledge, reprogramming my own mind, studying psychology, reading hundreds of personal development and self-help books of all kinds. All with the purpose of improving and reshaping my own life. So, how could things go so wrong? All I felt was a deep sense of hopelessness and anxiety. I was hurt beyond words, a broken man. I just wanted to disappear off the face of the earth. There was no way I was going to be able to get myself through this ordeal, again. This was it for sure, I was fifty now, really too old to move forward and start over and did I really want to? I just wanted to check out and leave this life. It was only a matter of when and how.

One morning as I woke up I had what I can only describe as an awakening. I had a block of thought, like a downloaded message from someone or something: "Getting beyond what is, becoming you." I sat up thinking, "What the hell was that?" Then I got: "Books you will write." I was shocked, where had that come from? I had never experienced anything like it before, and equally shocking was that I had never, ever thought of writing books before. But I loved sharing my knowledge, helping people deal and overcome challenging times to be the best they could be.

I spent the day just thinking about what it all meant. I was scared to tell anyone; for one thing, I didn't really understand it and for another, I thought if I told someone they would definitely think I was losing the plot with everything that was happening to me at that time. So, I kept it to myself. But I had never encountered such a feeling, such a sense of certainty and clarity about anything before. While trying to make sense of it, I noticed that my mood had changed – I wasn't feeling down any more, in fact I felt quite optimistic and hopeful. But the more I thought about the spooky message, the more I convinced myself that it wasn't real, it was my imagination, a dream and by the end of the day I had worked my way back into a state of depression.

The next morning, I awoke to: "I am your spirit guide, Isaac." My mouth literally dropped open. That was all I needed to believe that this was absolutely real. With that block of thought came an instant memory that made me understand the message so clearly. As part of my recovery from my suicide attempts in my twenties I went on a spiritual healing journey. As part of that journey I was told by a spirit healer that I had a spirit guide, and they would reveal themselves to me one day when I was ready. It was something I had long forgotten until that moment when the memory came flooding back, as clearly as if I was being told for the very first time.

I was now faced with a scary choice, do I continue with my plan to end my life or change course and choose to live. Also, if I live do I replicate what I can of my old life, salvaging what I could from the broken pieces, or take a leap of faith and trust the message and my spirit guide. It was whether to take up the challenge of the unknown hardship and struggle which could lead to discovering that there was something more to life and finding my true purpose and unconditional happiness, set against the known lesser discomfort which could lead to maybe even more struggle because I would never reach my true potential. I opted to follow my instinct to live and take my life back for the life I hoped could be.

I call this moment my awakening. I was on my knees, down and out, ready to bow out of life but, then also filled with a knowing that there was something more, something better beyond where I was at that moment. It was like my soul, my spirit cried out to me to take the next step in my journey, letting me know that finally I was ready to become the person I was meant to be.

But writing a book … and more than one; how would that happen? I hadn't the least bit of knowledge about how or where to even begin. And when I told people I was going to write a book although they didn't say it in so many words, I knew they thought I was crackers – to be honest there were days when I thought I was. But needless to say they did what all good families and friends do, highlight other options and possible things I should consider, namely go back to my old career and old life but wrapped in different words. It would have been the easier option; well, even taking my life would have been the easier option for me. But that message changed me. I didn't know if I could write a book or if anyone would be even interested in reading my book. But I would try.

Two years later and the answer is "yes I could" and it's called *Getting Beyond What Is: Taking back your life*. Funnily enough my challenges were not writing, with that everything seemed to just fall into place. Ideas popped into my head, offers to go to book learning seminars, invites to webinars to learn about how to write a book, all flowed seamlessly to me. It seemed like things just appeared as I needed them. Past experiences from my personal and professional life became so much more relevant as I began writing, it all made my path very clear.

My work wasn't learning how to write and publish a book. It was overcoming my depression, the shame and blame I tagged to my life falling apart when I knew so much and was so successful already, getting beyond the doubts and the fears of embarking on something new, rebuilding my self-worth, changing my life, starting over, believing I could do it and coping with the emotional baggage of it all were the things that challenged me every day.

The problems I was facing and trying to overcome were the same ones I was writing about and as I pulled myself back up, the chapters in my book were written. Everything I had experienced in my life, all the bad stuff (being bullied throughout my childhood and teenage years, suffering with deep depression for many years as a teenager and adult, suicide attempts and losing three businesses) as well as the good stuff (great relationships, lots of money, a loving partner, family and friends, and a highly successful corporate career) all seemed to be part of my great big life lesson.

I came to understand more deeply something that I already believed and that was: when you are inspired to do something, when it comes from a higher power you truly believe in, nothing that other people tell you will move you from the path of achieving that which they think is not possible.

The key to getting beyond your struggles is making choices that invite new possibilities – new ways of thinking, feeling, behaving and living your life for the better. However, when the hardship you've suffered in your past is still impacting your life now, you can't fully allow or accept new ways of doing anything. It only acts as an anchor to your past, keeping you stuck in a frustrating cycle of brokenness, that only invites a feeling of hopelessness into your life.

Let go of any regrets you have, since you can't go back and change anything, you have the choice of moving forward or continue struggling. Silence that voice of shame, because there is no shame in going through hard times. It's important to know that it's okay not to be alright through this difficult time. If you feel the need to hide your suffering somehow, you're harbouring feelings of shame about what has happened or is happening to you, which you need to let go of. Accepting your struggles as part of your journey will help you learn from them and that new knowledge will allow you to improve your life.

I've written this book, inspired by my own lessons and enlightenment to share with you the knowledge and advice I wish I had known when my whole world collapsed and I went through my struggles and dark times – what led to my attempted suicides, why I didn't really start living until I was twenty-six and how I fell back into depression all those years later. I've learned especially over the last few years that the reward for struggling is wisdom and I share with you also how I got beyond depression, financial ruin, homelessness and being down and out, to taking my life back and creating a wonderful new life that is independent of conditions, full of possibilities, joy and laughter, and knowing that all is well.

Writing this book has already changed my story and my hope is that it will help you change your life. I will show you that there is hope even in the darkest of times. That you can get beyond your struggles and hardships of your daily life, a life that has stopped working for you now, to live a life full of purpose, love, peace and happiness. When you take a chance and stand up, again, you realize that you are so much stronger than you were before and so much greater than you ever thought possible.

What if you just had to take one more step until you achieved what you're looking for? Surely that would be a step worth taking, even if you knew it would be a hard one to take. As you deal with difficult situations right now, know that better times are just around the corner and if you push past what you're going through, you can get what it is you really want.

When your life gets hard it's easy to stop dreaming or to scale back your dreams because it feels like they are unrealistic and un-achievable now. But, if you give up on your ability and power to make things different in your life and do what seems easy like complain, blame others and situations, worry be negative and doubtful, your life will always seem hard to you. But taking back control of your life and finding a way to become hopeful, optimistic and believe that what you desire and want is possible and the day is coming when everything changes, your life will eventually become easier and you will begin to see life as it was meant to be.

Dreams are bigger than your problems and I have learned that you should never sell yourself short just because things are not how you would like them to be right now. So, take the next step as it might be just the one that gets you beyond your struggle and to the life you desire.

" You can *do things today* that shape your unknown future. **MAKE EVERY DAY** the time when you *turn what you don't know* into *what you would like to happen.* **"**

—Michael Nulty

CHAPTER TWO

It Begins With You

We can all go through times in our lives when getting through difficult life events, such as a mental or physical illness, a job loss, bullying, financial struggles, divorce, break ups, the loss of loved ones, or some other traumatic life stressors gets the better of us. When our life feels all messed up and everything seems to go continually wrong. While some periods can be short, others can last for months, years even. It can feel like that's all life is about, a habitual circle of sameness and hard times with struggle becoming a permanent fixture, sucking the life out of our plans, hopes, dreams and ambitions.

What is even more difficult than going through hard times is resisting the daily temptation to give up, even when it feels like defeat is staring us in the face. But I've learned that nothing is ever as it seems to be and things are never as desperate as our thoughts and emotions lead us to believe. But what is more important 'is the fact that if you give up now, two, three, five years from now your life will probably be the very same. Nothing truly changes until you do.

When suffering hits, it can be difficult to understand it. In order to understand why it's happening and in an effort to get better quickly we often try to simplify the process and so underestimate the time it can take to get over it. But the truth is that although we may try, we may never truly get over some hardships or some painful experiences that have caused irrevocable changes in our life. However, you can get beyond those struggles by learning how to see and deal differently with the new realities in your life.

Creating your new better story begins with what you do now. Can you set aside what's happening right now and look beyond your physical reality to what could be and make the decision that this is the day when everything changes for you? It's going to come down to the power of mind and a battle of willpower: that part of you that wants to let go of the struggle and reach for a better life, against that part of you that's had enough, that's tired of fighting and is fearful of what an unknown future may hold, so it plays on your natural negative bias and keeps reminding you that you're far better staying just where you are.

You have to make a choice – accept ownership of what's happening and take responsibility for your life or allow misery to continue its reign for a few more years. You will come to understand better how you make those choices when you read chapters five 'The Power of Mind' and six 'One Mind, Two Sets of Rules'. Who are these two parts of you and where does their power come from?

Is life tough right now? Can you be open-minded enough to consider that it could be more how you are reacting to things in your life than what life is throwing at you? Have you ever thought about why sometimes minor situations escalate into more troublesome matters? Well you might be surprised to learn that a lot of struggle, past and present, is self-created. The situation or obstacle that triggers the struggle whether it's a family fall out, a bad relationship, a failed business, sexual orientation, addiction or maybe something different, only equates to a small proportion of the struggle. The rest of the struggle comes from how you respond to those situations. Do you choose to ignore the struggle, reject it, maybe accept and embrace it, or do you run from it completely?

I can certainly say that I have done all of the above and can see how those choices led me down certain paths and not others. Take some time to think about how you react to situations now. Has it always been that way? Look back at situations that you've gone through and consider what other possible outcomes there might have been, if you had chosen a different response. Would a different reaction have caused less pain for you and maybe added less drama to an already tough time?

How you react to things are learned behaviours over many years and they happen unconsciously. Every emotion that you feel has its own behavioural response. Being in a situation that makes you feel afraid will cause you to respond differently to being in a situation that makes you feel grateful. There are two chapters in the book that explore this in great detail and give you many answers and ways of changing your reactions to all things that come into your experience: chapters eight 'You Become Your Emotions' and ten 'Thoughts Become Things'.

When you look back, you see things from a different perspective and it's easier to see what you maybe could have done differently. Although it would be nice to go back and do things over, life only goes forward. The best you can do is to benefit from what you have learned and change what happens next.

So, anytime you feel a struggle entering your life, pause your reaction before your automatic response system kicks in and takes over. Step back from the situation and use the moment to think, and look at the struggle again.

Choosing whether you respond to the situation as a negative or as an opportunity to react with a new and different perspective sets in motion the course of what happens. When you turn from your path of usual responses and embrace a new way of doing things different opportunities come to you.

Moving forward from any difficult situation or time is not about grand gestures, which from my experience only seem to take you right back to where you were, but months even years later. It's about small steps and learning new ways and new things as you go along. You are always only taking your next best step, not allowing what you're thinking about – everything that's going on in your life, what has taken place in your past or what could happen in your future – to shadow your decisions. That type of thinking only creates a sense of fear and fear will always stop you from moving forward. It's just about one step forward, looking around for what you think and feel is the next thing that you should do. You are making strides towards what you want your life to be like, not for ever but for now, in this moment. Do you want this moment to feel better a little bit happier or do you want to stay in misery a little while longer?

It is so important to realize that your life is greater and bigger than any one moment and any one situation. You are not defined by what has happened or is happening in your life, now. The things that are problematic and appear troublesome now are just there to point you in a different direction. And believe me when I say that no matter how much you're hurting now, someday you will look back and realize your struggles today changed your life for the better.

Not that long ago when I made the choice to live and change my life, I still had to overcome many things before I could be well again. I was not only fighting the symptoms of my problems and depression, but also some deep rooted limiting beliefs and values, my own demons, my now very low self-worth and old mental programmes that needed to be aligned with the way I wanted to be. So every day I got up, I would declare that my only job, my purpose and all that truly mattered today was feeling positive. I would deliberately look for nice things to do and think about. I would focus only on the positive aspects of what was happening around me and ignored the negative by avoiding all negative conversations and any conversation that was about my past or future. I distanced myself as much as possible from all sad news and bad news. I had enough of my own to contend with and the fact is that your emotions are influenced by what's going on in the people around you and which emotions they're expressing. I made the commitment to myself that no matter where I was going or what I was doing, I would do whatever I could to feel that little bit better today than I did the day before.

I won't kid you, in the beginning it was pretty hard to do. I got shut down by my depression and fell short on many, many days, but I persevered, getting up every day for months with my philosophy that I didn't have to figure it all out today – how I was going to get better, what would my life be like in the future, could I be happy again – I was only interested in making now, this moment feel better and move on from there.

As I moved forward I started to experience the positive momentum of my own therapy work. The dark clouds and the hopeless days started to fade and although I had bad days when everything would come crashing down they were sandwiched in-between some good days. But as I started to put my life back together, like piecing together a one thousand piece jigsaw puzzle without knowing what you're trying to recreate, I came to understand and learn that there is a sequence, an order to the creation and manifestation of everything I encountered and went through in my life. I began to truly get it for the first time that I was only experiencing a version of what was going on around me. That my life in the physical outside world was a reflection, an expression of my mental inside world, made up of my fears, desires, hopes, dreams and life experiences, and the good, the bad and everything in-between. That what I wanted to have and what I had was separated by what my mind had come to know, believe and accept as possible. I could only see and experience life as I was, not as life actually was.

Your life will always be at its best when you live in the present moment. But you can be pulled out of living in the present when you are carrying the weight of the past with you in every moment. If you are like me and have suffered with depression, although you may not be cured of depression right now, you can learn to live as well as you can while you are managing and recovering from it. You have to accept that your life will not be the same as it was before, that what is done is done. You can't change the past or undo the damage from it. However, you can decide to live as well as possible despite your struggles and pain, and you also can move forward into a new and better reality from this point.

To embrace this new journey, get beyond your struggle and create your next new and better story, you will have to step outside your comfort zone, open your mind and yourself to the idea, the possibility that there are things in life going on which might be true even though you may not understand them or even use your five senses to verify them. So, forget who you have been, what you are not, where you were, what you had. None of it makes any difference right now. Your future reality has far greater things available to you than you have ever had before.

In the beginning it can be hard to wrap your head around the idea that what you think and do can have any impact on the hard times you're going through. But once you do, you better your life and change your future. You are not what has happened to you, you are what you choose to become now from what has happened.

Finding yourself and becoming aligned with who you really are is probably the most profound and life changing experience that you will ever encounter. It is the ultimate goal in life and when you find the way to connect with your own true self, your life takes on a different meaning. However, when you disconnect yourself from who you truly are in preference of the personality that society has caused you to portray, you live a life of separation from all that you have the potential to become.

We all wear a mask at some stage of our lives to hide who we are because, at times it's easier to be someone different in order to fit into an certain environment and situation. But if you're truly honest with yourself, you can never hide from how you see yourself, regardless of what you show to the outside world or where in the world you take yourself.

I know that as you read these words right now, through the eyes of stress, anger, depression, fear or the circumstances you are facing and going through, it may be difficult to believe them and to accept that tomorrow can be any better than what is occurring in your life right now. But I promise you that although it may not be visible, even seem a bit fantastical and ridiculous at this moment, there is a way, a real way to change your perspective, your reality and make your life good maybe even for the first time.

The future is unknown and largely that is true, but you can do things today, that will shape all of your tomorrows and that makes now a powerful place to begin changing your life.

" You can't change other people's behaviour that is their choice. But you *can* change how you REACT *&* FEEL about it. That's your choice and power. **"**

—Michael Nulty

CHAPTER THREE

The Other Side of Change

W e all on some level and at different times in our life, fear change. Often our fear of change, of the unknown is greater than our desire to achieve what we truly want. So, we spend time, energy and effort every day, working hard to ignore and avoid our unresolved destructive patterns and issues. Hoping that if we can keep everything we don't like or want under wraps, and plaster over the cracks of all that isn't working in our life, we can postpone or even avoid the changes we need to make. We play it safe, become a settler, a creator of a restricted and reduced life experience. We diminish our desire, even become angry at ourselves for needing more. We talk ourselves out of wanting something because we haven't figured out how to get it. Sound familiar?

Change is an integral and constant part of life, whether you embrace it or resist it. It's part of who you truly are. From the moment you arrived on this planet you began transforming, adapting, learning and evolving into the person you are now, and will become. Every time something changes, you grow and discover new insights about who you are and your true potential. You learn lessons even from changes that did not turn out the way you hoped they would. Change triggers progress, moves you forward to different and better choices, allowing you to re-evaluate your life, and look at things from a different perspective.

We all want more, it is a natural aspect of who we are as human beings. We all have situations, areas, conditions in our life we wish to improve, receive more of, and make better. Whether it's our financial situation, our relationships, our working conditions, job prospects, our health or our appearance. Different people want to make different changes for different reasons. Improving parental skills may be an area for some people, whereas desiring to be the owner of their own business may be the goal of others. Change is part of the order of making ourselves and our lives feel better and feel good. After all, when you think about it, isn't everything you want and desire – material objects, good health, loving relationships, peace, money – wanted and desired because of how it will feel once the change has occurred and you have it!

Change is relative and dependent upon your own personal perspective. Losing twenty pounds may be a lot easier than gaining a promotion at work, similarly making more money may be more difficult than finding love. What you will come to know is that everything is relative to where you stand or rather where your mind is set on the multitude of things you wish to change and bring into your life experience.

Have you ever wondered why some people succeed in changing lots of things about their life quite easily, while other people struggle and end up creating even greater conflict than before? Getting to the other side of change is a mental journey, first. It's the journey of preparation, acceptance and focus. Bringing your thoughts, feelings and beliefs up to speed with the transition, the crossing over, the exchange you wish to bring into your experience. Do you deserve it? Do you believe you can achieve it? Do you truly want to be better? Maybe remaining in a state of misery feels safer because it's what you know now, even though it's not what you truly want, the idea of having to change can make you think that it's the way your life is supposed to be. So, you remain stuck, unable to move forward.

Branching out into the unknown is extremely unnerving. Allowing change back into your life can be difficult. It's hard to let go of old memories of past changes which didn't lead to the most pleasant experiences. Removing the resistance to what's holding you back can make you scared, causing you to return to the familiar feelings of your old reality. Creating a false sense of the past and altering the reason, the purpose you set out on the journey of change in the first place. Real positive change sometimes starts with unsatisfactory situations, times of hardship and suffering. I know from my own journey that my transformation and the important changes I made to my life required me to accept uncertainty, embrace the unknown and trust that everything would work out for my greatest good.

When I look back at my own life now, with a new understanding and appreciation for my past, I realize that all the changes regardless of the outcome, and there were times when I changed aspects of my life to make it better only to end up making it worse, were intrinsic to the person I am now. I recognize that so many great experiences occurred as a result of the decisions I made to change things in my life. Each of my career shifts, working across dissimilar industries, five countries, three continents and thousands of diverse people gave me the opportunity to see the world, gain new skills and confidence. Changing so many aspects of my life to recover from my many years of depression all brought a new way of feeling, thinking and living my life today.

Change brings new beginnings and excitement to life. As human beings if we didn't adapt and seek out new ways of doing things, life would be extremely predictable, uninteresting and extremely boring. Think for a second how different your life would be if our ancestors chose not to invent anything, or not to embrace new inventions. How different would your life be today! You may not think of yourself as an inventor, but you are. You are an inventor, a creator of your own reality experience, whether you know it or not at this point in time.

To grow, to get beyond what you already know and past your comfort zone, you have to be willing to feel awkward and uncomfortable doing things for the first time until you develop a new comfort zone and a new level of appreciation and understanding. It is said that the person you are not right now can help you discover the person you truly are. And that when a problem in your life comes into greater clarity it causes you to create a solution that did not exist before.

Very few things will change overnight and all the things you want to change won't happen all at the same time, which can create a lot of frustration and annoyance because you can't see the physical evidence of the changes quickly enough, although you can feel the emotional pain of the change. It makes you start to question whether it will happen at all.

You add the greatest delays when you usher in new things, before you have healed and put your past about those things to rest. It could be starting a new relationship when you still hold hurt from a previous one, or earning a lot of money when unconsciously you still hold an old poverty mindset. Preparing yourself for the change is crucial otherwise you get caught up in the physical and emotional struggles of the past and the present, instead of giving your attention and focus to where you are going and the outcome that will create in your life. Be patient while you go through the process of changing your personal story. Change begins in its smallest form first and so you may not notice it in the initial stages, but it is happening.

Today can be the day when you no longer just dream of a better life, but start making your life the reality you want it to be. Changing your life for the better is something that you can only do for yourself.

Getting Beyond What Is

A greater life begins when you change your own self first. What I know for sure is that nothing will change in your life for the better, until you begin to alter how you see what you have and how you think about what is absent from your reality right now.

A better life is a life that feels good to you. It can be a life full of material objects, a bank account full of money. A life of peace, love and harmony. It can be a life of freedom, where the past no longer decides what you do and who you are. Where the future no longer scares you. It can be a state of being, a sense of oneness with life, knowing that whatever comes your way, you have the ability to get beyond it.

When you trust in yourself, the guidance that comes from your source and the universe, your connection, your relationship with life changes and everything you desire to make your life what you want it to be, comes to you freely.

" Don't underestimate what you think you can do. Change can bring *new* SKILLS *&* CONFIDENCE *in your abilities* that you couldn't see before. "

—Michael Nulty

CHAPTER FOUR

The Reality of It All

Have you ever thought about why you and your friends can experience the same thing at the same time, although you can have very different responses to it? Well, the simple answer is that we process the information coming from that experience, or occurrence in different ways using our own unique internal processing filters, such as the memories of our life decisions, our beliefs that act as our personal truth, our self-identity that is linked to our past selves and a value system that is most probably out of sync with what is important in our lives now. These filters all interact with each other at different levels within our mind, influencing what we get to experience in every moment, creating our own unique perspective.

We all go about our lives as though we are living in an objective reality; that everything we see, touch, taste, smell and hear is present in its fullest form, that we experience the total version of each occurrence. But it is all really an illusion of our mind. What you see or the way someone looks at you. The words you hear and the way those words are said to you. The touch and texture on your skin of something or someone. The smell of aromas around you and the taste of your daily food. These are all processed to create an internal representation of an outer occurrence, but not the entire occurrence itself.

Two people can look at the same situation or attend the same event, maybe the cinema to see the latest blockbuster and one will love the movie and tell all their friends about how great it was, while the other argues that it wasn't all that great and continues to point out the bad acting and rubbish storyline. I remember getting my first car, an old Ford Fiesta, it wasn't a great looking car and I'm sure it looked pretty crappy to some people, but to me it was a sense of freedom and independence.

Have you noticed that depending on your perception of what's occurring in your life, you can be negative and gloomy, or carefree and optimistic? Every perception is about you. The pathways you choose, the changes you make, whether it be change to your job, your appearance, your house, your friends or your relationships are altered to fit with your perspective of your reality. Even a beautiful sunny day can be annoying and frustrating if you are feeling unhappy, worried or suffering with depression. The governing law of reality is that if you don't perceive something, it doesn't and can't exist in your reality.

The Reality of It All

The way your reality is, or is not, is totally dependent upon you, your notions, expectations and attention upon what is happening in your life. It forms the basis of your reality and although there may be a lot going on in your life which is probably pretty good and really the way you want it to be and would like it to continue, what is becomes primarily concentrated on all that is missing, absent or has not yet appeared in your reality. Your daily conversations to others and your own self-talk becomes about what is wrong, and how much you don't like what is wrong and how long you've been living what is wrong, even joining groups that are also talking and agreeing about what is wrong.

Every day you beat the drum of what is happening that is not working, whether it's something as simple as the weather, your job, your car, your kids, your family, finances or health you slowly become blinded to the good things that are happening all around you. You become stuck noticing everything that is not the way it should be with either all of your life or just aspects of your life, not realizing that really everything just exists now and your happiness and good feelings are acquired between and around what is happening – both the good experiences and the bad ones. How you perceive your reality is vital to creating positive change.

Reality is your perception of it, and your life is how you perceive reality. Although reality itself consists of all things, past and present, conceptual or tangible, it can't be objectively experienced because there is no reality beyond the perceptions or beliefs you have about reality. Your reality is represented, and comprehended from how your mind organizes, identifies and interprets the information collected from your sensory devices or what you call your five senses. The reality you experience is merely an internal portrayal generated by your mind of reality itself.

It is common sense to think that reality is what your eyes, ears, nose and fingertips present to you. But your visual, auditory, kinaesthetic, olfactory and gustatory senses are really not able to provide a sufficient description of your surrounding environment. They essentially are the devices with which you collect data from all the outer stimuli in your world. Think of your body as the border between your mind and the outside world, your senses are the outposts.

It is your mind that brings about the meaning by enriching the sensations themselves with further details. Your mind is the producer and the director of the reality you are living right now. It controls and manipulates how you perceive, interpret and experience your environment. It brings order to it, makes sense of it. It defines how you see your life, the choices you make, the reactions you take and the results you produce.

The perception creating process is quite an amazing computational feat by your mind. It subjectively appears effortless because the processing happens below conscious awareness, making you oblivious to what's going on. It begins with what's called an outer occurrence, something happening outside of you, causing your five sensory devices to receive tiny pieces of sight, sound, touch, taste and smell or stimulus by means of light, sound or another stimulant. The input energy or data gets transformed into neural activity and transmitted to your brain. Before it is internalized it gets washed through your all-important life filters which limit and modify the data that is included in your view of the occurrence.

Your internal processing filters of your memories, beliefs, self-identity, values and attitude function under the rules of what I call your mind's gatekeeper. Actually, its technical name is Reticular Activating System or RAS. Its job is to regulate on average over two million pieces of data flooding your senses every second by reducing the streaming data to a more manageable amount for your mind to process through a cleansing ritual of deletion, distortion and generalization.

The deletion process plays a vital role in dramatically limiting the amount of information that reaches cognition. Any sensed data that has no relevance to or importance for your attention gets deleted. The remainder of the sensory data gets either distorted, making misrepresentations of reality, constructing imaginary futures by altering some data to fit a certain theme, or generalized which is one of the ways learning occurs. Information you have already stored in your mind is taken and used to draw broad conclusions about a subject, occurrence or stimulus. The downside of drawing conclusions is that it can take an individual occurrence and turn it into a lifetime experience.

Once your gatekeeper has executed its series of calculations and screened the data through your primary filters, the remaining sensations of approximately forty to fifty thousand data bits get magically pieced together. Resulting in the mental recreation of the stimulus, and your perception.

To create sustainable change in your life you have to understand what filters are operating in opposition to how you wish to experience your life today. A lot of your values and beliefs have been passed on to you from your parents, society and early childhood. Therefore, you keep active the things that were important to you and what you used to believe, and so choose what you experience in your now reality. How you react to something in the present can actually be a response to memories organized in a certain way around a certain subject from your past. Your attitude, whether positive or negative, is just a learned tendency from what you have experienced and observed, but now causes you to evaluate things in a certain way, manifesting the outward behaviour you display.

The whole filtering process is highly complex and you don't really need to understand how it does what it does. But it raises important questions for you to consider. Would the vast amount of deleted data have provided a different version of reality for you? Did opportunities get deleted, even distorted because of what you believe? Have you placed a high level of importance on what you are trying to achieve or is your old value system of unworthiness still in operation? Could it be that your filters are out of rhythm with the reality and life you wish to receive? Restricting and blocking your efforts to move forward to your new and better story.

Reality as you perceive it to be, begins inside your own mind. A happy, joyous, abundant life is technically created through vast sets of connections and maps joined together via chemical and physical pathways, making up your mindset and perception on an array of different subject matters. You have become accustomed to trusting what you see and know, but not so much trusting in what is unseen and unknown. Everything is essentially here and now, in various states of visibility and invisibility with your mind constructing the reality you are perceiving. There is no such thing as the unknown only things that are temporarily hidden.

It's probably difficult to comprehend and accept right now that you are a translator of what's happening around you, or what I call a perceiver of reality. However, it's not your job right now to try and figure it all out. Everything will make sense as you learn and understand more about the workings of your mind. Getting to know your mind in a new way is a process. You start by opening up a little bit to the idea and possibility that you are greater than you think you are. By allowing yourself to accept, maybe even for the very first time that there could be more to life than you may know, believe and have experienced before this moment.

Every day, your life is shaped by forces you may not even realize exist or indeed are part of you. Your reality is only an interpretation of the world you live in. Life can only be how you perceive it to be, but beyond what you see and understand as your present reality lies an alternative version of life. A life that is mostly unknown and in-accessible to you right now. But when your perception shifts, your personal story shifts, and the reality you experience changes along with it to fit your new perspective on life.

Nothing can change in your outer world until it changes in your inner world. You can change your job, you can change your appear-ance, your possessions, your spouse, you can change everything that is physical in your life, but if you don't understand and change what's happening in the world of your mind, you will continue to fight the same battles every day. Your reality can be different, even though you can't perceive it physically right now.

" You can't change things by **FIGHTING** your current reality. You change them by *thinking in a new way* that makes your *reality change.* "

—Michael Nulty

CHAPTER FIVE

The Power of Mind

The concept of mind is understood in many different ways by many different people and by many different cultures. It has amazed and baffled people throughout the ages. Although Aristotle, Plato, Freud, Jung and many other leading mind gurus formed varying theories on the mind, there is no one single, universally agreed upon definition.

Our mind is implausibly complex and nowadays it's become even more difficult to figure out not only what is our mind, but also what is the difference between our mind and our brain. People seem to just use the words interchangeably to mean the same thing. However for me, and from my many years of research into the power of the mind, I have come to understand and accept that while our mind and brain are intertwined and share some of the same characteristics, they really are conceptually very different.

Getting Beyond What Is

Our mind for the most part works through our brain. Our brain essentially provides the perfect apparatus, the biological circuitry, through which our mind carries out its duties and principal role of decision maker. Our brain is that physical organ in our body, that intricate mass of grey and white matter in our head that we typically see in pictures.

However for me, our brain is not our mind. The mind is not an organ, nor is it a physical entity. It is the awareness of consciousness. The ability to know what we are doing and why we are doing it. It is part of the invisible, mystical world of thought, emotion, feeling, imagination and love. Intricately interwoven into our body's brain, interacting seamlessly as a whole for the entire duration of our life.

Do you believe your life can get better? Do you believe you can change the way you are? Do you believe you can respond to situations to give you a more favourable outcome? Do you feel you are worthy of receiving better things in your life? Your answers right now may be 'no', but that is only because of how your mind has been set. When your mind is set to possibilities, your entire consciousness expands to show you that you are greater than you know and have come to believe you are. However, when your mind is set to scarcity and limitations you will feel struggle, discord and restrictions in creating any positive impact in your life. Most people fail to create any long-term change in their life or harness the power of affirmation, the Law of Attraction because they haven't yet come to understand how to take back control of their mind and wield its power to create the change they now desire in their life.

What you believe, how you think about things, the opinion you hold of others and yourself, how you behave, the habits and patterns you have formed, all operate according to their own specific rules and commands within the world of your mind. From the very first day of your arrival on this planet, you began compiling information, converting your surroundings into meaning, and forming conclusions, which now pretty much rule your reality.

Your mind never stops working and although you experience outwardly a physical and material life, you really do live in your head. The amount of time you spend thinking, predicting, analysing, procrastinating, dwelling on things and weighting up the pros and cons of situations is phenomenal. You think about everything; you have views and opinions about everything. And although you may not share them outwardly through words and gestures, they are very much swirling around in your head. Even as you read this information your mind is at work assimilating it, rinsing it through what you believe, comparing it with memories you hold on this subject that might correspond or not, and weighing up the importance and value on knowing such information. Essentially, your mind is trying to make sense out of everything you are reading.

Although your mind and its component parts are changeable over time, certain aspects won't embrace change easily and so will fight back to stay exactly the way they have been created. Changing things in your physical life, without first eliciting the cooperation of your mind to decode what has most probably taken you a lifetime to create, is next to impossible. A change of mind is an inside job, mental work precedes physical action because your mind will reject and delete any information being received that is contrary to how it has already been programmed and wired by you from your life experiences.

When I read my first Louise Hay book You Can Heal Your Life over twenty years ago, in 1994, I rejected the book completely after reading just the first chapter. I really couldn't understand what it meant, at that time. All that I could hear was my internal chatter, my existing beliefs judging the information and concluding with the thought of "what a load of mumbo jumbo, it is not the truth as you know it to be". However, a few months later, I found myself drawn back to the book and as I began reading it again, I was astonished to discover that my mind this time was more open to receiving the information.

To read the book I had to be patient, uncomfortable at times and disregard a lot of what I already believed as the truth in favour of information that I really couldn't comprehend at that moment. But because I placed a high value on making my life better, I accepted being mentally uncomfortable in order to gain these new insights and bring about my own positive change of mind. At times it felt as if my brain was going to burst. I could nearly feel my brain processing the new knowledge and dumping the old. I took the time to read the lines, paragraphs and chapters slowly and carefully. Reading them over and over to really get my mind to comprehend the full meaning and intent, eventually, in time everything made sense and it did indeed change the course of my life.

We all have a unique mind, with unique thoughts, feelings, perceptions, memories, beliefs and attitudes, accompanied by unique sets of configurations shaping the flow of information inside our head. Your mind can set you free but at the same time can incarcerate you. When you come to know and understand what your mind does, how it does it, and why it does what it does, you can start to make the necessary corrections to the world within, dismantle your mental blockers and bring into your life experience the happiness, health, success and abundance you desire, and indeed deserve.

As you go through the shift from something familiar to something unfamiliar you will naturally feel conflict. You will experience doubt and hard times, even become fearful of the change. Many people when they meet resistance to changing a mindset that no longer serves them, unlearn what they have come to know and understand about their life and give up the struggle to create something new and better either too easily or too early. So, try to release any anger you might have towards yourself or indeed life, if you can't see the physical evidence of change quick enough, or if you fail to make the changes you want all at the same time.

There is no miracle to creating a change of mind. It takes time to alter what has taken you many years to create. Changing your mind's existing rules and laws, deconstructing deeply embedded programmes, altering filters, habitual thinking patterns that now operate and feel like your own personal prison, won't happen overnight and it won't happen at all, unless it is done with a new and different perspective.

You will find that some days changing how you think and feel about your life will seem easy. Some days will be all about the mental battle between the new and the old way of doing, thinking and feeling. Some days will just feel hopeless and not worth it. What you don't know is that there is a mental reason or rather a different mental attitude towards these different days operating just outside of your awareness. And recognizing 'why' is the key to successful mind change. Is it that you are just tired? Are you not seeing the change and desired results quick enough? Are you focused upon the things that are in opposition to what you want? When you uncover and know the 'why', you reveal a piece of what is your mental blocker. And knowing and dissolving your mental blockers allows you to make better choices for your life.

Choice, an awareness that you have options and the knowing you can think differently creates a change of mind and a greater perspective on the unseen, magical world inside your head. Every thought leads to other thoughts of a similar nature creating a more positive mood and a new and improved behavioural response to the things coming into your life. Increasing the frequency of what might seem inconsequential small mental changes every day in favour of what you want and away from what you don't want to manifest will generate positive momentum and a more permanent change of mind.

Through your mind you have the capacity to go beyond the present, transcending time, space and reality. So, is your mind just an earthly bodily meaning producer attached to an organ called your brain? Or is it far greater than just a sense converter and instructor, with the ability to transcend its human host into a realm of spirituality? A conduit between your body and spirit, between the physical, material world you live in and the non-physical world beyond your physical earthly senses' capacity to perceive.

You get to make your own mind up! Let's continue on this journey of discovery and creating your new better story.

" Life will *bring you better* when you *focus on better* and **BELIEVE IT'S POSSIBLE**. You can only *experience* what your mind is *prepared to accept.* **"**

—Michael Nulty

CHAPTER SIX

One Mind, Two Sets of Rules

Understanding the make-up of your mind, how it works and how you can better make it serve your new better story and the life you wish to receive is easiest to comprehend when you divide your overall mind into two different aspects: a conscious mind and an unconscious mind. Or what I call in the context of change and making your life better: your thinking mind and your reacting mind. Both aspects offer their own set of attributes, dynamics and rules.

Your two minds although working to different protocols operate in tandem to make your life work the way it does. Your conscious mind is the part of your mind that you are probably most familiar with. It is your awakened state, the part of your mind that is aware of what's happening around you right now, in this moment. It represents who you are now: who you call 'me'. It is the part of your mind that engages with the world around you through physical gestures, movements, speaking and writing. It is where you think, focus, use hindsight and foresight, even present judgement. But it is the many known and unknown beliefs, values, habits and memories held in your unconscious from your past experiences that influence and guide those decisions.

When your conscious mind and unconscious mind are in harmony, you have true power. What you think about and the corresponding reactions take you in the direction of your goals and ambitions. You are of a single mind, with a feeling of oneness. However, when your two minds are in opposition to each other there is a feeling of discord and a tug of war.

For example, you make the decision that you need to change your job. You consider the advantages and the disadvantages of moving to a new job and it makes sense that a new job, with better prospects and more money is just what you need at this moment in your life. That's all conscious mind work, thinking things through making conscious decisions. But now you start to hear from your self-worth: have you got the right skills, are you good enough? Your beliefs: will someone hire you, the economy is quite bad so will you really get more money? Memory: you did a lot of interviews for your last job, the 'no you're not suitable or not qualified' for the position was heard a lot and then starting something new, meeting new people created some anxiety. All of this additional information is coming from your unconscious mind bringing a different context to the decision to getting a new job. It can really do a pretty good job of convincing you that maybe where you are is better for now. Does that ring a bell with you?

So, how do the two different parts of your mind do what they do? Well, as you have already discovered in chapter four 'The Reality of It All', your overall mind controls how you perceive and in turn experience things in your life. Your conscious mind is the leader; it's the captain of the mind ship. It communicates a request and your unconscious mind or what you could think of as the mind crew, then goes to work on making it happen from the simplest of things like walking across a room to playing a concerto on the piano. Or it will provide you with all the reasons why it can't carry out the request.

What is important to understand is that you cannot remember anything stored in your unconscious mind or bring past conflicts into the present without your captain giving the order, that is, your conscious mind choosing to think about them in the first place.

Your two minds do similar things but they do them very differently. Your unconscious mind is subjective; it doesn't think or reason independently unlike your conscious mind which you now know can be objective, theoretical, set goals, work out 'what if' scenarios and think things through. Your unconscious is the powerhouse of memory and will process all the data it receives from your senses. However, your conscious mind has limited memory and will only process and store five to seven pieces of data at any one time. Your unconscious mind is only present in the here and believes that what you're thinking and talking about is factual and happening right now, because remarkably it can't tell the difference between what is real and what is pretend. To the contrary, your conscious mind is able to decipher the difference between the two. It is a mind of directing and making choices with the ability to focus, imagine and think in terms of not only the present but also the past and the future.

The best way to get a picture of what your minds are like is to imagine an iceberg. Your conscious mind is the pinnacle, the part of the iceberg that you see and appears to float on top of the water but as you know that is not all of the iceberg. There is a lot more underneath the water which is not visible; actually it's a whopping ninety-one per cent more. So just like there are different levels to an iceberg, there are different levels to the mind with the unconscious part being the most challenging to understand. So let's deep dive a little and examine why it has such power and how did it come about.

Let's be clear, your unconscious mind is not working against you on purpose. It's actually the part of your mind that keeps all of you running and alive, operating all of your bodily functions 24-7. And because it wants you to be able to manage much of your daily routine with ease, it hard-wires and automates many of your daily repeated actions, forming habits so that it doesn't get bogged down with unnecessary processing of the same stuff. If you repeat something often enough it will get automated. So, what may start out for you as meaningless action can become bigger, greater and more embedded into your unconscious mind forming a habit, a behaviour, an attitude and a reaction.

Have you ever experienced driving your car for a distance say on familiar routes, only to arrive later at your destination without having any conscious awareness of driving for part of the journey? Your unconscious mind did all the work, navigated the traffic, changed gears and avoided colliding with other vehicles. Quite powerful stuff, and quite scary! Don't you think?

Your unconscious mind is your own personal super computer. With a colossal sized hard drive. Holding a database of memories, experiences, beliefs, values and programmed responses all coming from your life experiences. It's quite hard to believe but so much of who and how you are today stems from the early years of your life.

Your conscious mind only began developing when you were around the age of three and then not fully developing until you hit your early twenties. But your unconscious mind, that mind that believes everything is real and happening, was ready to go from the time it was formed before you were even born. And during the critical and early formative years of your life without the benefits of a fully developed conscious mind, your unconscious mind began doing its job by absorbing and filling up your unconscious empty vessel with content from the world and society you were born into. Converting your surroundings into meaning and forming your own personal storehouse of content and an endless cycle of counterproductive beliefs, values, habits and attitudes.

Getting Beyond What Is

The majority of what you experience between the time of your birth and the age of six or seven follows you from your childhood into adulthood. For example, "Oh, you're a bad child", "You will never amount to much", "You're just an average achiever", "You're good at nothing", "Money doesn't grow on trees", or other such statements, became truth to your unconscious mind, creating a printout in your life, consistent with what you have come to accept as real and your own personal truth. If the things you were told and the personal encounters you experienced as a child happened as an adult and were not true, your conscious mind would discredit the source and the information would never make it to the unconscious mind and into your present day experience.

But just because you don't remember something doesn't mean it's not presenting itself in some shape or form in your life. The memories of some things are closer to the surface than others and are therefore more easily streamed to your conscious mind. They are the things you focus upon on a regular basis. For example, if I were to ask you to recall what your phone number is or indeed what problems you have at work, then you could easily bring them into conscious thought quite quickly. However, things that you give less importance to or traumatic experiences in your life are stored a bit deeper down in your unconsciousness and as a result need greater focus and concentration to remember and bring into conscious awareness. Sometimes to get to the root of a deep problem you need to attend therapy sessions where over time the therapist can help you dig up those roots so that they have less power over your life today.

Memories of experiences deeply affect your perception and personality. Your reaction to something in the present can actually be a response to memories organized in a certain way around a certain subject. Every significant emotional event, pleasant or unpleasant you have gone through is stored in your mind's memory bank. It has memorized all your comfort zones and it works to keep you in them. It will do everything it can to make anything new fit into the mental maps and patterns that already exist on that subject. It will cause you to feel emotional and physically uncomfortable whenever you attempt to do anything new or different, or to change any of your established patterns of behaviour. You can feel your unconscious pulling you back toward your comfort zone each time you try something new. Even thinking about doing something different from what you're accustomed to can make you feel tense and uneasy. However as you continue to repeat something, thoughts or actions, your mind will create new pathways and the more you continue to reinforce this new way of thinking and acting the more dominant and natural this new way will become.

Making any change to your life, must begin with awareness and mindfulness of the differences between the two aspects of your mind and how they operate and present themselves in your life every day. Change can only happen in the present. When you make the decision to be more aware of your thinking, feeling and behaviour you can make different and better choices to align with how your life is to be now. When something happens and you feel the internal mental struggle entering your life, pause, take a step back and give yourself a moment to think and look at the struggle again. Remind yourself that you can now choose a different way to react to everything that comes to you.

But remember when you forget to be conscious, your unconscious mind gets back in charge again, and you revert to the old way of doing things. Imagine your conscious mind as a flashlight in a dark room. It will illuminate specific parts of the room but will never show you everything in the room or remember anything once the light has been moved to a new illumination point.

Reconfiguring and deconstructing deeply embedded programmes, altering filters and habitual thinking patterns won't happen overnight. It's also difficult to stop the streaming of your past into the present, your judgemental thoughts and personal criticism coming from your unconscious mind. But you can break the cycle by not reinforcing existing patterns and habits of thinking.

It will take time to create new rules, associations and links that will serve how you want your life to be now. When you think you can't change your prevailing beliefs, habits, attitudes, values or self-worth, remember they were made by you at one point in your life, therefore, you really do have the power to change them.

"DON'T GIVE UP if you can't see things working out and changing physically right now. *Change begins in your head before you ever see it in reality.*"

—Michael Nulty

CHAPTER SEVEN

What Do You Believe?

There was a time when you believed everything was possible. When you were inquisitive, innocent and your mind was only bound by the limitations of your imagination. Every day was filled with excitement and eagerness for more. You lived a life where happiness and joy were independent of conditions, where doubt and anxiety had no place and meaning in your life yet. The present moment was all that you really cared about. It was a time when you truly believed that all things were possible. And although time has put many difficult experiences between you and those days when you believed you could be anything, do anything and have anything you wanted – you can believe again in possibilities.

This is a scenario for you to think about and work through as you read this chapter about beliefs. Take a situation in your life at present, something that you're trying to make different and better.

Something that maybe you've been trying to overcome or change for a while now, but you just haven't been able to make it happen. Now grab a piece of paper and write down what you believe about it. What are your core beliefs about this particular situation? So, now answer this question: What would be possible if you believed something different about this situation?

Your beliefs are at the centre of who you are and discovering what those beliefs are and how they play out and impact you and your life in either a positive or negative way is an essential part of your journey to creating your new and better story. It may be a belief you hold about your personal identity, your abilities, skills or lack of them, a belief that you're not worthy, not lovable, not attractive enough or maybe it's one of the many beliefs you have about your financial situation, or something different.

The decisions you are making right now and everyday about your life are based on your beliefs about your reality, and the possibilities that exist in your reality are defined by your beliefs. Many of which you may be surprised to know were established during your childhood, with other beliefs leftover from situations and circumstances that are no longer relevant, but continue to serve, restrict and limit you from making the changes you want in your life now. Beliefs that were once useful to you to some degree, may now be the same beliefs that imprison you and keep you away from achieving all that you desire and want. When your beliefs support and align with what you're trying to achieve, there is no resistance because the roadblocks have been eliminated.

Nearly twenty-five years ago, I came upon a little card in a store that said read: 'Reality is the product of your thoughts. What you believe will come true for you.' The simple inspiring words on a card put me on a path of exploration into the power of the mind, beliefs, positive thinking and creating a new reality. I was excited by the idea that if I changed my thoughts and beliefs, I could change my life. Although I was very drawn to the words, I really couldn't comprehend how your reality, your life could be shaped or impacted by what you thought about or indeed what you believed.

As time passed and I became distracted and too focused on the stuff of life, the saying faded into the background of my mind, until one morning while I was writing this chapter of the book, the saying just popped into my head, like an old friend saying hello. The meaning so clear and profound; the essence of how I live my life now. I didn't know it then, but the card was a helping hand on my journey through life and something I desperately needed at that time. But it would take nearly another twenty years for me to truly know and understand the importance, relevance and consequence of not just my thoughts but my beliefs about who I truly am.

You may not know this but beliefs essentially are an on and off button for your ability to do anything in the world. If you don't believe you can achieve something, you won't have the opportunity to find out if you can or cannot. What you believe may be dissimilar to how you think about things now. But have you taken the time to evaluate the difference. So, before you allow your life to be dictated or even sabotaged and impaired by what you presently believe, it is important that you know and with time understand your beliefs and why you believe what you believe.

By as young as six years old, your belief system was already well formed by your very open and accepting unconscious mind. What you learned and experienced to be right and wrong, fair and unfair, good and bad had formed as a belief. What is more astonishing is that research shows that these early formed beliefs are not likely to change a lot throughout your adult life. And so they sit actively and inactively in your unconscious mind, showing up from time to time in your life experience. It's worth taking a moment, maybe even grabbing a pen and jotting down some of your beliefs about what you're trying to make happen in your life at this time.

We all know that beliefs are powerful, wars have been waged, religions have been built, people have suffered and died because of their beliefs. But what are beliefs. Well, a belief in simple terms is a thought that is true for you, it lives in your unconscious mind. It's where you think something is real and a feeling of being sure that someone or something is true and exists with or without you having experiential evidence to verify the certainty of it. Beliefs are your personal Laws and you have many different types of beliefs on many different types of subjects. They are like a web all interlinked together, one belief supports another and another and so on, which is why they are so powerful. They are built upon a mix of fact and fictitious perspectives and prejudices, and they allow you to reach conclusions about situations despite evidence to the contrary and making logical sense.

Once established, beliefs are accepted as fact and are rarely subject to scrutiny even by your conscious thinking mind. When you believe in one thing, you will usually disbelieve in anything that's contrary to the core belief. They hold as your truth and anything to the contrary, gets wrapped in doubt, dismissed and rejected by your mind. Everything you see, experience, think and feel is adjusted to fit with your beliefs.

So, how do you know if the beliefs you hold, are limiting, sabotaging and producing negative consequences in your life? Well, the best place to begin is to look at the areas of your life that you've put considerable amount of effort into changing, but even though you've tried and tried you continue to struggle to make the changes you want. It's most likely you are operating a limiting belief stopping you from achieving the success you require with that situation. Any action you take will have next to no effect until you take the time to correct the belief or introduce an opposing belief on the subject.

In my previous career, I talked quite a lot about beliefs and one thing that always stood out to me was that people didn't realize that they were free to choose their beliefs. The beliefs that are now operating in your life may have been inherited from a variety of sources, your childhood, culture, society, family and experiences. They may be serving your life very well or they may be putting up roadblocks to where you're trying to go, but that doesn't have to continue. You can choose to believe something different about every situation you wish to change.

Once you've identified a new belief you have to go about installing it in your unconscious mind. You have to immerse yourself completely in the new belief until your mind accepts it as one of its own. The methods that I and countless others have found the most effective are visualization and affirmations. Affirming out loud, looking at yourself in a mirror, adding emotion to what you're saying is a much stronger way to say affirmations than just repeating them in your mind. Using your powerful imagination to picture your new better story, free from any barriers is one of my favourites. It also creates a lovely feeling because as you imagine with your conscious mind, your unconscious mind believes that everything is really happening right now. In chapters nine 'Your Emotional Shift' and ten 'Thoughts Become Things', I outline a lot more about how you can change your thoughts and beliefs. In chapter sixteen 'Creating New Beliefs', I take you through my process of changing limiting beliefs.

New beliefs simply allow possibilities to exist where they didn't before, which in turn not only changes your behaviour and emotions but also how you go about living your life. For example, if you hold a belief at the moment for whatever reason that says something like "I am not lovable", "Relationships are hard", "Love can hurt", you are most likely going to struggle to find a loving partner and relationship. However, if you work on changing that belief you open up the possibility to finding true love in your life because you have removed the barrier.

The same with money. If you have a belief at the moment that you will never have money, "Money is hard to come by", "I am always struggling to make ends meet", that is what your reality will be like, because beliefs can be self-fulfilling prophecies. However, work on modifying and then changing the belief and you remove the barrier, and the thoughts of earning more money and having enough money become a real possibility and something you now believe can happen.

But changing your belief won't magically make a new lover appear or lots of money appear in your bank account. You still have to work on manifesting those things, but it's easier when there are no belief barriers to what you want. Now it's a matter of committing to the changes you want to make – you may need further information or to learn how to do something new, but once you've accomplished that the change begins to happen.

Over the years of my life, I had to modify, change and add many new beliefs and allow old beliefs just to fade away. To write this book, I had to root out my limiting beliefs about my being able to write a book and introduce new beliefs. That's the thing about beliefs; old beliefs can fade when you recognize that a belief, something you've held from a very young age, may not be the truth you once thought it was.

What I've also learned is that changing a belief takes time. There is a myth that you can change a belief in hours and days. It would be great if that were the case but I don't believe that or rather I have never experienced that in any of my situations and experiences. Creating a new belief or forming a new mental habit can meet with quite a lot of resistance as you may have already experienced. It is suggested that it can take anywhere between thirty days and two months but it can take even longer than that depending on the belief. Some people go through hypnosis to reconfigure their unconscious thoughts to reflect what they want to believe. Mind you, although it appears to work for some people, I am yet to be convinced of its longevity in creating real change to a belief.

We can forget that the beliefs we're trying to change have been around for a long time and can run very deep within us. We have put a lot of time into creating them over the years and we most probably continue to breathe life into them every day too. Because beliefs come as part of a web of beliefs, when you start changing one the others will rise up to offer a challenge to that change. That doesn't mean they can't be changed, it's only a matter of time. Set the right expectations and continuing practising your new belief until you feel no resistance.

As you go through the shift from something familiar to something unfamiliar you will naturally feel conflict. Don't give up if you can't see the physical evidence of your new beliefs and your new array of possibilities quickly enough. It's difficult in the beginning to believe something that you can't physically see or really comprehend, especially if you come from a way of thinking that you will believe it when you see it. Most of us look inside our frame of knowledge and can only relate to what we can verify, test or see through our senses. But, and this is a big but, if we want to change things and be the creators of our future, and not live our life by default, we need to believe first and then I promise you will see. Remember what I learned many years ago: what you believe can become true for you.

" You are only defined by your ability to IMAGINE, DREAM and BELIEVE. When you grow and evolve you blossom into the greatest difference in your own life. **"**

—Michael Nulty

CHAPTER EIGHT

You Become Your Emotions

Emotions run so deep within everything we do and everything we are that they are one of the hardest and most challenging aspects of change. Our emotions can contain endless numbers of thoughts, although they are not as exact and don't make as much sense as thoughts. Nevertheless, they still add another level of complexity to emotions, which can turn into beliefs. Emotions and how they make you feel are the driving force of your life. So I've dedicated two chapters to emotions - this chapter which is talking about how we can unintentionally become our emotions and be that angry, sad even depressed person, and chapter nine 'Your Emotional Shift', which explains how we shift from being that angry, sad person to that happy, joyful and loving person we want to be.

One of the greatest lessons I've learned over the past two years and there have been many, is that my happiness is not dependent on anything or anyone. That happy is something I can become, just like sad and then depressed was something I became. My beliefs about happiness were that it was outside me, in that it was in what I did, who I was, where I lived, how much money I had and what designer labels I wore. It was something I learned and came to believe from my early life – happiness had to be constructed in the physical world for me to feel it in my mental world. But the challenge with that is I had to continually acquire more and more, and refine my ideas of what I did because regardless of what I had and who I became, the joy factor didn't remain constant and diminished as the years went on. Today, I find happiness and contentment in some of the most simplistic things because I have learned how to build my happiness from within myself.

I think it's fair to say that we can all at different times of our lives, peg our happiness onto things outside ourselves or indeed something which may or may not happen in our future. We have come to accept a belief about happiness that when we have the perfect job, relationship, money, house or whatever, we will be happy. But it doesn't work that way. We have to be happy for happiness' sake and everything will come to you from being happy.

There is always an emotional bias to whatever you're going through at any one time. If you are feeling anxious you will probably pay more attention to threatening situations coming into your experience than say someone who isn't suffering with anxiety. Likewise, if you're suffering depression your outward focus will be more on the negative things that are happening in your life and you become blind to all the positive aspects of your life, which seem to just vanish.

For example, when you experience difficult times in your life, you start considering and predicting what might happen in the future. Your mind becomes preoccupied with a series of negative 'what if' scenarios about a fictional future that has not yet taken place. The realness by which you experience the imagined outcomes, propel you into a world of feelings and emotions. A world where your stomach heaves with worry, your heart palpitates with fear and your breathing races with apprehension. A world where you can live for weeks, months even years feeling angry, frustrated, fearful, hurt, lashing out at people in a volatile way and wishing people, things and conditions were different. Sound familiar?

Emotions are a huge part of everyday living and because you are naturally emotive, over the course of a day you can be touched by a vast array of feelings and emotions. You connect to them in such a way that they create a whole new world around you and change your reality depending on how you are feeling at any given moment in time.

Emotions have the power to make your life work well or make you feel as if you have a life that is not worth living. They offer a motivation and zest for life and an equal opposite pessimistic and depressing perception of the same life. They bring you together with things you desire and push you away from sometimes the same things. They are the ultimate reason why you continually want and not want things in your life. When you feel good in yourself, you're able to shrug off even the most burdensome of tasks, but when you are feeling miserable, you view even an enjoyable activity with a sense of doom and gloom.

Emotions and feelings are crucial to your ability not only to adapt to the challenges of your daily life but to fully experience all of your life. Think for a moment about what your life would be like without emotions. It would be unchanging, dismissive and robotic. Even negative emotions play their part in helping you connect and get along with people in your society. How would you get along in society if you did not care at all how you behaved in front of your family, friends and co-workers? What would your life be like if you couldn't anticipate tomorrow with a sense of optimism and hope? What if you could never feel happiness, fall in love and be loved or indeed express yourself outwardly in the variety of different ways which, make you, you?

It is very common to confuse emotions and feelings. They are often thought of as being one and the same. In everyday language people use the two words interchangeably which shows you how closely connected emotions are with feelings. However, although they are related and refer to aspects of your human condition there is a difference in how they both serve you and play out in your life. They are like different sides of the same coin. However, the feeling of an emotion is a process that is separate from what causes you to have the emotion in the first place.

Understanding the different component parts of your emotions is key to creating a life that feels good to you on all levels. Living well begins when you learn to cope with the feelings your emotions deliver more effectively, instead of ignoring and suppressing them. Your senses tell you what's going on in the outside world, while your emotions which exist inside you tell you what these events and circumstances mean to you.

Emotions are a well-orchestrated set of alterations in your body which have the job of making your life more survivable by alerting you to danger, taking care of opportunities or something in-between. They involve different components, such as subjective experience, cognitive processes, expressive behaviour and psycho-physiological changes. You know when your emotions are active because they create very noticeable physical changes in your body. They cause your heart to race, the nauseous feeling in your stomach, the lack of saliva in your mouth, the tightening of various muscles, the quickening or slowing of your breathing, or some other biological change in your body. Emotions happen unconsciously to varying extremes in response to stimuli – some objects or situations outside of you. Even thoughts about something real or simulated will arouse your emotions and kick start the whole chain reaction process. Therefore, emotion can be produced by a thought, memory or external motivator.

Feelings on the other hand operate on a conscious level and are a mental portrayal of what's going on in your body as your mind interprets the emotions that become active within you. They are the next thing that happens after your emotions have been aroused and can range anywhere between extreme pleasure and extreme discomfort. When you feel emotions you form your own very unique perception of what is going on with you. They are conscious messages, insights into what's going on with you in mind and body. They will assist you in changing unhealthy behaviours, decoding important messages coming from within, they will help you accomplish greater things and create a sense of harmony and peace in your life.

You feel the world in so many different ways: from the warmth of the sun, the aches and pains of your body, the positive feelings toward a sunny day and most importantly your intuition, that gut feeling you have about things, people and situations. I think of these gut type feelings as the urge to do one thing over another to go one place and not another; as messages from my higher self, my source, my authentic self, the energy consciousness that is my spirit. These feelings are always guiding you to your greatest life and are intrinsically linked to your human emotions. Feelings give you a way to care, not just to think about the things you want in your life.

The word 'feeling' has upwards of twenty different meanings, depending on the dictionary you consult. However for the purposes of this chapter, feeling refers to something experienced as part of an emotion. While emotions cause you to feel, the feelings when experienced can trigger further emotional reactions. Your emotions are also influenced by what's going on in the people around you and which emotions they're expressing, causing emotional contagion. If you've ever felt moved to cry watching a sad movie you know the effect others' feelings can have on you. Also when other people are stressed or anxious, they can trigger a sense of anxiety and stress within you, prompting a never-ending cycle of painful and confusing emotions which produce negative feelings, which cause more negative emotions and a continually changing mental state, without you really ever understanding and knowing why.

Feelings about any situation or object are very rarely straight forward. They are multi-dimensional, consisting of a mix of different emotions and different emotional intensities. For example, if you are faced with starting a new job, you might feel excited, nervous or even fearful. Getting married or having a child might be marked by a wide variety of emotions ranging from joy to anxiety. These emotions might occur simultaneously, causing you to be somewhat overwhelmed by an occasion and causing you to behave in a certain way, or you might feel them one after another, making them much easier to process and express.

Your emotional sensations, coupled with your perception of what is going on in your body, trigger perhaps the most familiar component of emotions: the expression of the emotion itself. Expressive behaviour is the outward sign that an emotion is being experienced. This can include the likes of a flushed face, tensing of muscles, facial expressions, tone of voice, rapid breathing, restlessness or some other body language. Your body movements, gestures and posture reactions are based upon your feeling and its subjective meaning linked to the emotion that has become active within you.

We all spend a significant amount of time interpreting the emotional expressions of the people around us, so that we can better interact and communicate effectively. Our ability to accurately understand these expressions is tied to what psychologists call emotional intelligence and these expressions play a major part in our overall body language. When you are feeling an emotion, it's often written all over your face. At a basic level, when we notice people smiling it tells us that there is some level of happiness and pleasure being experienced, while a frown indicates some form of sadness or displeasure. According to experts on what is called the 'facial feedback hypothesis' of emotion, the expression on your face can influence your emotional state. When you activate the muscles that control your facial expressions, you actually trigger internal changes that lead to the corresponding mood. If you frown, you'll feel mad. If you turn the corners of your mouth down, you'll feel sad. And if you turn the corners of your mouth up in a smile, you'll feel good. As the song says, to make 'grey skies clear up' just 'put on a happy face!'

However, as I am sure you have come to know by now, interpreting emotional expressions is a lot more complex than just understanding what a smile and frown means and putting on a happy face. For some people disguising their feelings has become a way to exist and to live every day. When I was going through my own depression I became an expert at masking what was really going on inside me both mentally and emotionally. Leading to the rise of self-destructive behaviours and suppression of my real feelings.

An important aspect of emotions that we forget about sometimes is the chemical elements which are produced when you are having an emotional experience. When your body comes under any type of change regardless of your age, race or gender, it stimulates the production of a wide variety of chemical responses. The endocrine system typically triggers glands to release chemicals known as hormones into the bloodstream, binding to receptors to transfer their message to cells. Another response is for the brain to prime nerve cells to produce neurotransmitters or chemical messengers, which send impulses to neighbouring cells throughout the nervous system. Together, hormones and neurotransmitters send messages to reach every cell in the body, working in harmony to provide total wellbeing.

Chemicals are a natural component of emotions and are produced by your brain and body. They help to control you, adjust how you respond to things and effectively alter your mood. For example, if you sense danger the stress hormones, cortisol and adrenaline will be released in response to the potentially fearful and threatening situation. Once the alarm to release the hormones has been sounded there must be a physical release of them in either fighting or running away, which is called in psychology your 'fight or flight' response.

There is no one happy or sad chemical and which chemicals are used vary from situation to situation and emotion to emotion. But it is worth knowing more about four chemicals that influence your happiness and play a role in making your life better. The easiest way to remember them is by the acronym DOSE: Dopamine, Oxytocin, Serotonin and Endorphins.

Dopamine is a neurotransmitter and most commonly associated with the human pleasure system. It provides feelings of enjoyment, motivating you to do or continue doing certain activities. It's more associated with anticipation rather than actual happiness itself. It provides natural highs that you experience from looking forward to things, such as eating chocolate cake, going on holiday, socializing and all other pleasurable activities. Low levels of dopamine can result in loss of satisfaction in life and the usual things that once were pleasurable and can bring on periods of depression.

Oxytocin is released through closeness with another person. It's a sort of bonding chemical and is very much present for periods of intimacy. It can also be triggered through social bonding, eye contact and attentiveness from another person. Some people call it the cuddle hormone.

Serotonin is essentially the calming chemical. It makes you feel watchful, attentive, focused and relaxed, keeping your mood balanced. If you are in a good mood you've got serotonin to thank and if you are not, you have serotonin to blame. It's estimated that eighty per cent of serotonin exists in your gut and is governed by your state of hunger. So it probably explains why your mood changes when you eat or when you don't.

And so finally, the fourth chemical – endorphins. Endorphins are produced as a response to certain stimuli, in particular pain, stress or fear. They are morphine-like chemicals that help diminish your body's pain while at the other end of the scale trigger positive feelings. They are sometimes referred to as the mind's 'feel good' chemicals. They are responsible for your feeling of pleasure and euphoria. These feelings of pleasure exist to let you know when you've had enough of a good thing, like food, wine, sex, companionship, etc. If you are into exercising you will no doubt have experienced the natural high you get after working out. Endorphins will only last for short periods of time in your body.

The purpose of chemicals and hormones is to step-up or step-down your brain's activity level. However, what is important to know about chemicals whether they be hormones or neurotransmitters is that the reason the chemicals are released into your body in the first place is to do with what's going on with you.

To understand how you can better manage, take charge and make changes to your emotions and the whole chain reaction, I have to take you back to how your subjective feelings, bodily responses and expressive behaviour came to be the way they are now in your life.

Being human we are all created with certain programmes pre-installed in our body and unconscious mind so that we can survive, flourish, procreate and, eventually, transition from this life experience. The intuitive and instinctual nature of emotions gives us an early warning of impending threats or dangers in our external environment. Our primary emotions, the likes of fear, anger, sadness, joy, disgust, trust, anticipation and surprise, are programmed in a certain way by nature and then modified through our own subjective life experiences, which ensures no two people will ever feel the same way about the same situation.

Meaning, your emotion of joy and mine although of the same origins will be physically expressed differently, based upon our own subjective meaning of what is arousing the emotion in the first place. World renowned emotions psychologist, Professor Robert Plutchik considered there to be eight primary emotions – acceptance, anger, anticipation, disgust, joy, fear, sadness, surprise. And that all other emotions, of which there are many, come as a combination and a derivative of our primary emotions. Similar to the way an artist mixes primary colours to create all the other colours in their palette.

As you live and experience the environment you are born into you encounter many unknowns. And as the objects in your world produce emotions within you, those emotions and related feelings even your expressive behaviour begin to accumulate in your unconscious mind's memory bank. From sensations as subtle as your likes and dislikes to stronger sensations of curiosity and fear. As the unknown object is given a name, it becomes something of meaning to you. And it is through this process that emotions and feelings become paired with thoughts, mental images and attached to every object you come into contact with, making your emotions more about how you have learned to respond to the environment and situation you were born into rather than how you would presently react. When similar objects, situations, events are experienced repeatedly you form an emotional conclusion about how to live life and, more importantly, how to survive physically and mentally in the world around you.

Since early childhood, when you were allowed to shriek with pleasure or howl with anger you've learned to rein in the outward expression of your feelings. You learned to regulate your emotions according to the situation and society you were born into. This resulted in certain emotions being expressed differently or stored in your unconscious mind through repression or some other form of self-deception. Your true feelings about your life and yourself are kept under wraps, ignoring the valuable messages and sabotaging your emotional wellbeing from your unconscious mind.

Like them or not, deny them, suppress them all you want but emotions and feelings are very much a part of you, just like your eyes, nose and ears. Emotions don't stop, because once you get used to a situation such that, over time, it affects you less and less, you become bored. Then your human instinct and need for more, drives you to seek more stimulation and change. Wanting, desiring more is a natural human trait. Without it the universe would not expand and the world and indeed people would not be what they are today.

The teachings of Abraham-Hicks were very instrumental in changing how I looked at emotion and there is a wonderful quote which I think sums feelings and emotions up quite well, it says: "Feelings are much like Waves. We can't stop them from coming but we can choose which ones to Surf."

"Pay attention to the messages coming from feeling. Ignoring something SMALL today could mean you have to deal with something BIGGER tomorrow. "

—Michael Nulty

CHAPTER NINE

Your Emotional Shift

It's easy to get all mixed up when you begin exploring the world of emotions and feelings for the first time. And contrary to what you might think emotions are malleable and can be changed and modified by altering the various different components that make up your overall emotional experience. For example, shifting your attention from what you are observing, and re-associating your feelings with certain external situations and stimuli. You can choose to focus on a more positive aspect of a situation, rather than being fixated on the problem. Walk away from an abusive argument. Or change your expression and behaviour; if you smile or frown you will notice slight changes in how you feel. Just the act of laughing can bring forth a happier feeling. Reappraising any situation will lead you to emotional change. It doesn't happen overnight as you didn't create everything overnight. How you choose to live your life has tremendous power over the way you feel every day.

I found that the best way of getting to grips with my emotions was by putting them into some order. When you put emotions or anything really in your life into some form of order, you remove the mental chaos and bring some sense to everything, which in turn makes you feel a lot calmer and in control of what's going on mentally. By challenging your thoughts, beliefs and unconscious programmes you can change your emotional reactions. Once you start to pick apart the illogical basis of your emotional associations you can free yourself from being dominated by the maladaptive emotions of rage, jealousy, rejection and dejection, and instead boost your adaptive emotions of happiness, contentment and joy.

Think of your emotions as being positive, pleasant and giving good feelings. Or negative, unpleasant and causing discomfort. While the clearest distinction is that negative emotions feel very different to positive emotions. Different emotions feel different from each other; embarrassment feels different to sadness, which feels different from fear. Joy feels different to hope, which feels different from contentment. All emotions can be placed on a scale between extreme pleasure and extreme discomfort, with a zero point between where neither positive nor negative feelings are experienced, such as the way surprise is often experienced.

I recommend using the emotional scale created by Abraham-Hicks. It is the emotional guidance scale that made most sense to me and which I used to gauge where I was in relation to feeling better emotions when I was going through difficult times and my depression. It is by no means the only emotional model or scaling system out there. If you find it doesn't work for you, go in search of one that resonates with you, as your ultimate goal is to find a way of making your life better continually, not just on the odd occasion when conditions are a certain way.

The emotional scale is a series of twenty-two emotional variations that will help you work from feeling bad to feeling better about whatever you are going through in your life as you move more towards pleasurable feelings and away from painful feelings. At the very top of the scale are joy, love, knowledge, empowerment, freedom and appreciation. Number two is passion. Third on the scale is enthusiasm. Number four is positive expectation and belief. Five is optimism. Six is hopefulness. Seven is contentment. As you move into the emotion at number eight which is boredom, you should now be aware that the feeling of being bored can lead you to being pessimistic, which is number nine on the scale. Number ten is frustration, irritation and impatience. Number eleven is feeling overwhelmed. Twelve is disappointment, while thirteen is doubt. Fourteen is worry. Fifteen is blame. Sixteen: discouragement. Seventeen: anger. Eighteen: revenge. Nineteen: the feeling of hatred and rage. Twenty is jealousy. Twenty-one is the feeling of insecurity, guilt and unworthiness. And finally, twenty-two is fear, grief, depression, powerlessness and the state of victimhood. I have placed a full list of the emotional scale at the end of this chapter, which will help you pinpoint where you are emotionally on every subject you're looking to feel better about. When you identify and label the active emotion you bring awareness to what you're feeling and the opportunity to explore the reason why it's being aroused. You can't make your emotional shift until you recognize and name the emotions you're feeling.

The emotional scale concept is a simple one, well, simple to explain but obviously more difficult to incorporate into your daily life. Your job is to identify the emotions that are causing you the greatest disruption and negativity in your life. You begin by choosing an unpleasant situation that can trigger an emotional response within you and notice how you feel about it. Start with your basic emotions; does it feel more like anger, sadness, happiness or something in-between? Find where you are emotionally on the scale so that you know what your emotional state of mind is right now regarding the matter you're trying to feel better about. When I did this for the first time, I was surprised by how much I couldn't tell the difference between some emotions. Disappointment felt like sadness but it wasn't sadness. But, like me you will eventually get the hang of identifying your feeling towards everything in your life.

For example, let's take money as being the object that arouses the emotion within you. You may feel worried, anxious even fearful about your financial circumstances. And so every time money comes up in a conversation or even in your thoughts, it triggers your emotional feelings about money. Worry, anxiety and fear become how you feel about money, "I'm worried about those bills", "I'm afraid I won't be able to pay the mortgage" and so on, you get the idea. And because you convert a lot of feelings into thoughts they become limiting beliefs about money in your life.

The emotional scale is just a barometer to allow you to see where you are in relationship to other emotions. The idea is to work through the reason you are responding to the different subjects or objects in your life the way they are and move through the feeling of the emotion to a more beneficial and less disempowering one. For example instead of worrying about money, feel frustrated about it and then on to being contented about it and on to positive expectations about money.

The process initially will make you feel uncomfortable and of course you will have feelings about the emotions you are feeling. But allow yourself to fully feel the emotions without criticism or the sudden urge to change them. When you have a painful emotion the likes of fear, anger or anxiety, stop feeling and bring your feeling into a thought where you can examine it more: "Why am I afraid, angry or anxious about this?" Thinking about and not just feeling the emotion will give you information about why you are feeling and reacting the way you are. Are you responding to situations and circumstances in your life with fresh emotions or through your automatic emotional response system, hard-wired from repeating the same emotion and emotional response over and over again? Chapter ten 'Thoughts Become Things' will show you how you can use your thoughts to examine in greater detail your emotions and feelings, and how different thoughts and thinking patterns can help reprogram your mind. Chapter eleven 'Positive Changes', will take you through techniques that will help you shift your emotions.

In the process of getting to know your feelings, your coping skills will be put to the test. You will obviously find yourself actively pursuing the very thing that for years you avoided which, in itself, is a frightening feeling. Have patience and persevere, you will get there.

When you are down, it feels sometimes like you have to stay that way. But the truth is you can change how you feel by choosing what you do. You don't have to be fearful of what might be around the corner or depressed about what your prospects for a better life may be. When you realize you're the only thing standing between you and a greater life, you get motivated to take action. That's the thing about emotions and feelings, you can't sit around waiting for them to change. You have to do something to change them.

THE EMOTIONAL GUIDANCE SCALE*

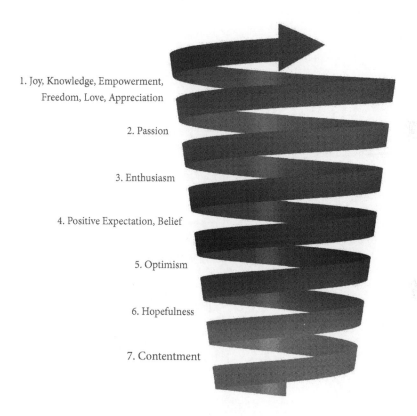

1. Joy, Knowledge, Empowerment, Freedom, Love, Appreciation

2. Passion

3. Enthusiasm

4. Positive Expectation, Belief

5. Optimism

6. Hopefulness

7. Contentment

Upward Sprial

*Emotional scale by Abraham-Hicks

Downward Sprial

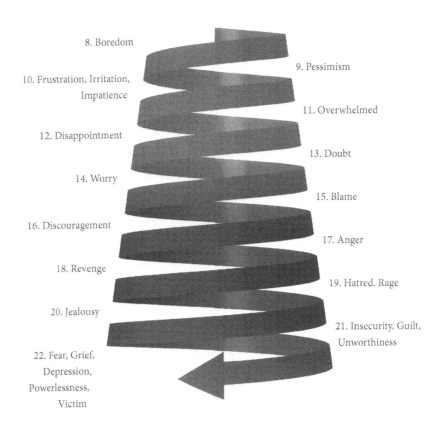

8. Boredom

9. Pessimism

10. Frustration, Irritation, Impatience

11. Overwhelmed

12. Disappointment

13. Doubt

14. Worry

15. Blame

16. Discouragement

17. Anger

18. Revenge

19. Hatred, Rage

20. Jealousy

21. Insecurity, Guilt, Unworthiness

22. Fear, Grief, Depression, Powerlessness, Victim

" Hard times can cause your life to unravel. You can find yourself somewhere you never thought possible. But you can RISE UP and LOVE LIFE again. **"**

—Michael Nulty

CHAPTER TEN

Thoughts Become Things

There is no better way to begin the journey of making your new better story come to life than through your own thought stream. You think and feel your life into existence every day. The thoughts you think based on the beliefs you hold and the emotional feelings you attach to them create the overall vibration that you transmit to life and the universe. But you can choose to think differently about your life, have different thoughts and create different feelings by telling a different and better story about your life now and how you want it to be.

Your thoughts and thinking patterns are the windows into the mystical and somewhat magical conscious and unconscious world inside your head. It's important to recognize the true power of your thoughts, as it is through your thoughts that you can explore and modify your own mental patterns and find many ways by which you can improve and learn how to dispute and replace thoughts with ones that allow you to create a better overall life experience.

A thought is an idea, an image, an opinion produced by your thinking. It is not an instruction nor is it a feeling. It may not even be true or real. Thoughts arise randomly from everywhere as your mind interprets and brings meaning to the world around you. Thoughts are the birth of many of the beliefs you hold today. The beliefs that limit your change, hold you back, were once just a thought. But over time they formed beliefs about what you can and can't achieve, and who you can and can't be. But as thoughts have the power to form beliefs they also give you the ability to examine those beliefs, talk about them, dispute them, decide if you agree or disagree with them and create new beliefs.

You have thoughts about everything, positive ones, negative ones and thoughts that are neutral. You have views, opinions about every aspect of your life, your friends, co-workers and your family's lives. You even get in touch with your emotions and translate them into more thoughts by describing the feelings they generate in greater detail. Not surprisingly, you mostly have the same thoughts about the same things every day.

You never stop thinking just like you never stop breathing. As soon as you stop one thought, your mind generates another one. Do you know you have over three times more thoughts than you take breaths in a day? It's estimated that you have fifty to seventy thousand thoughts a day versus an average of twenty thousand breaths a day. Your thoughts begin the moment you wake up and don't stop until you go to sleep. Even when you meditate you have some level of thought, although meditation does help reduce the velocity of your thoughts and thinking quite considerably. But you can never really stop conscious thought until you sleep.

As you learn more about your thinking patterns, you realize your thoughts can trap you in feeling strong negative emotions. For example, it is common to blame another person's behaviour for your own feelings. You might say to yourself that the other person "makes me angry" or "upsets me". But really the other person doesn't magically control your feelings. You make yourself angry, upset, even depressed through your own thoughts, words, beliefs and further feelings about the situation and the other person, and what they may or may not be thinking, saying or doing.

You may not have realized before that your thoughts affect your feelings. Most people assume it's the other way around; that feelings come first and thoughts naturally follow. But as you observe the relationship between thoughts, feelings and emotions, you begin to recognize that the influence works both ways. Although thoughts make you feel and feelings make you think, they are very different in how they play out in your life.

The next time you are asked "how you feel about something", take notice of your answer. For example: "How do you feel about depression?" If you reply with something like "It can devastate your life", you are replying with your thoughts and beliefs on the subject, not your feelings about depression. A feeling answer would be something like, "I feel disappointed that there is such a stigma" or "I feel grateful that I was able to get better". It works the other way round too, where you might give a feeling answer to the question: "What do you think?"

As you have read in chapter eight 'You Become Your Emotions', your thoughts can trigger your emotions. Learning how to think thoughts that are about how you want your life to be and not about how your life is right now will most definitely improve not only your feelings but also your emotional state of mind. You don't have to be held hostage to your emotions. Become aware of the thoughts that precede strong emotional outbursts and by altering the thought stream you'll find that you can better manage and influence the behaviours that tend to follow negative emotions.

While learning how to modify your own mental thinking patterns is possible, it's not easy. Your thinking patterns run deep and you have been under the influence of the type of thoughts you think for so long that they have become your norm. They are now well-established habitual thinking patterns which are deeply embedded in your unconscious mind. In fact, they are so deep that right now you may even feel or think that a lot of your thoughts are just fine. However, just knowing that you can think differently creates a change of mind and a greater perspective on the unseen, magical world inside your head.

All your thoughts have some reason for coming forth into your conscious thinking mind. Some thoughts are voluntary and you create them consciously, some are intrusive coming from your sudden attention to something in your environment, some are automatic, some more about association and programming, and some are unconscious and instinctual.

Thoughts can also be of a spiritual nature, bringing forth messages and guidance from your inner self or your source, very similar to the way your feelings bring forth emotional and spiritual messages. Thoughts translating into messages beyond the physical human you is, of course, something that can only occur when you fully embrace and connect with that part of you that is non-physical and which I call spirit. But it is known by many other names, some of which I have mentioned throughout this book, such as inner being, soul, inner self, source or higher self.

What you think about influences and shapes not only your day but also your entire reality. However, not all thoughts are wrong and need to be altered, very much like not all of what you believe is limiting your success in life. You can choose not to bring past conflicts into the present by not thinking about them after the initial thought. The stream of judgemental thoughts and personal criticism coming from your conscious and unconscious mind is difficult to stop. But you can stop adding to the existing pattern and habit of thinking, and in time break free of the negative thinking. The thoughts which should interest you the most and the ones you need to begin changing, are the thoughts that drag you down, reinforce old limiting beliefs and values, trigger emotionally negative feelings and make you think the opposite to what you want your life to be now.

Every thought you think leads to other thoughts of a similar nature, creating your thinking pattern loop. By being observant you can learn so much from the thoughts that seemingly just pop into your head. Becoming aware of the thoughts that cause you to feel miserable and by letting go of fruitless lines of thinking, you learn to adapt and change your thinking habits and escape the trap of unproductive habitual thinking. This allows you to become free to think thoughts that deliver more productive and more harmonious outcomes to every situation.

As you probably know and have experienced before, once a thought stream gets going on a particular topic, it gains momentum and can last your entire day, making a significant impact on your mental health and your ability to function in many different ways. However, if you pay attention to your thoughts you can do things to manage and control them to some degree.

Focus shift is a good technique to use. It is also a good method to use to help destress when you're struggling to come up with solutions to problems. You distract yourself from certain thoughts by thinking about or doing something different. The purpose of shifting your focus is to temporarily get your mind off whatever is causing you to become stressed. Whether it's something physical that's aroused emotions of anxiety, worry or fear within you or just a stream of negative thinking that's having the same effect; here are some of the techniques I use:

▶ Find something mindless to do, like playing a game of solitaire, watch a funny video, clean your bathroom or kitchen cupboards.

▶ Instead of doing something mindless, switch to doing something that engages your mind, but in a different way. Do a crossword, read a chapter of an inspiring book or positive quotes that inspire you. The goal is to perform a pleasant task to increase some positive energy.

▶ It takes only a few seconds to recall a nice positive uplifting moment that's happened to you previously and to switch your thinking to this new scenario and subsequent thoughts and feelings. This is about using visualization to help you disengage from streams of negative thoughts.

▶ Walk away, take a break and literally go for a walk or run. Changing your physical behaviour will trigger thoughts about what you have switched your attention and focus on to, along with releasing endorphins which are a natural feel good chemical.

Choose the distraction that works best for you. But you need to practise the technique and be relentless with your efforts to make the changes. I use focus shift and distraction still to this day. After I categorize a thought as a thought that I don't want to be thinking about, say a thought that is linked to a limiting belief, I use distraction in a few ways. I quickly recall something that I've enjoyed doing in the past twenty-four hours so it's still quite fresh in my mind and not too deep in my memory bank. If you try to access events that are not at the top of mind you will find it difficult to bring them into your conscious mind quickly enough to make a difference. Remember, any memory that has an emotional attachment to it will be easier to recall than something that doesn't. Another way I use distraction is to just say, "Hey you (the thought) stop bringing me down" or "Thanks for that thought but I am choosing to think differently today", and I state what I want instead, or "Thanks for letting me know I still have unfinished business with X situation/emotion".

It's a matter of shifting your thinking onto something different to create a different stream of thought and reactive emotions. If the old unwanted thought comes back just repeat the exercise. You will eventually find that your mind gets the message and stops allowing the old thoughts to manifest. Remember, as I outlined in chapter six 'One Mind, Two Sets of Rules', your conscious mind is the leader, it's the captain of the mind ship. It communicates a request and your unconscious mind or the mind crew goes to work on making it happen.

If your thoughts become too much and the subsequent feelings too hard to bear, you can stop the momentum by taking a nap or slow it down by meditating. When you sleep, all momentum stops. But it will all start again right where you left it, if when you awake you go right back to the same thought stream. The idea of taking a rest is to give yourself a new start and an opportunity to gain more control over the avalanche of negative thoughts that can be overwhelming.

To change the things you think about, you must expose them to conscious scrutiny, that is, you must observe them as they pop into your thinking mind. A good way to keep track of what you are thinking is to keep a journal. When you see things written down, you can scrutinize them a lot more than trying to adjudicate them in your head. This kind of exposure to what you are thinking will provide greater clarity on the way you use thoughts to not only upset yourself but also create negative thinking streams and blocks of thought.

There is no way you can change a limiting belief until you recognize that it exists and your thoughts are the ideal window to view these beliefs. Do you ever think that life is unfair and that you are just unlucky, good things just don't happen to you, you're always in the wrong place? These are limiting beliefs and your mind will continue to collect evidence to support these beliefs, even if they're holding you back and stopping you from succeeding and making successful change in your life.

Your mind will always be biased towards the information it has already amassed about a specific subject, which is why somethings can be so believable. However, new beliefs will come and allow possibilities to exist where they didn't before as you think new and better thoughts. Thoughts start out as just thoughts, but they can become so much more because they touch everything in your life. Your thoughts can truly become the things you want in your new and better story.

"You *see* the way you *think and feel* about yourself and your life. When you change the QUALITY of your thinking you change the QUALITY of your life. "

—Michael Nulty

CHAPTER ELEVEN

Positive Changes

Many people think that the first step to moving forward and building a better life is action. But before you can change something with physical action you have to believe you can mentally. If you don't believe that something can be changed and made better your actions hold very little credibility and you mostly probably will struggle to make any real impact on what you're trying to achieve. Getting your thinking right before embarking on your next chapter will make your actions more effective and powerful. It is vital that you make sure that you haven't been sucked into thinking you can't achieve what you want before you start off on the journey of making it happen.

You are not hard-wired to think the same thoughts in the same way for the rest of your life. Thanks to neuroplasticity you can learn to create new neural pathways and make new neural connections so that you can break free of the habit of being your old self and a life that doesn't serve your needs any more.

Positive self-talk, affirmations and visualization are very good ways to start changing the internal and external negative dialogue that you have going on inside your head. The same mind that allows you to think the thoughts that limit your life can produce further thoughts, words and images that can help you refute your streams of negative thinking, create new steams of positive thoughts, modify limiting beliefs and create new ones to serve your new life and your new way of thinking and feeling.

Let's start with something that most people are familiar with: affirmations. Affirmations are merely sentences aimed at affecting your conscious and unconscious mind in different ways. You may have associated them with positive thinking but they work in op-position too. Many people use affirmations in a negative way with-out realizing it. They continue to repeat things like "I am not good enough", "I am ugly" or "I am fat" and the list goes on. Where do you think so much of our negative and crappy beliefs and thoughts come from? Not surprisingly because we say such things, we believe them. They have what I call the believability factor.

There is a bit of a catch to affirmations, and if you have done affirmation work in the past you may have found that you gave up the discipline of saying the affirmations long before the affirmations could get to work changing old beliefs and creating new ones. The reason for this, as you've learned in chapter six 'One Mind, Two Sets of Rules' is because your mind will reject anything that you don't already believe unconsciously. When you say an affirmation like "I am beautiful" or "I love myself", your mind will argue with you, based upon the story you have stored in your unconscious mind about your appearance, your self-worth and what you believe about that statement. The answer you tend to receive is "No you don't" or something to that affect and the reason for that is because your new positive affirmations don't have the believability factor. That is, they don't have it, yet.

The key to making your mind work with you is to start off with what I call soothing positive self-talk and not straight in with full on positive affirmations which can for some people be hard to do, especially if you want to stand in front of a mirror and declare them right to your own face. You can also combine them together. It's about finding what works best for you on the beliefs you're trying to change.

Soothing positive self-talk is about making a series of soft positive statements. They are more general than affirmations and rather than in the present, which triggers your conscious mind to dispute them, they are worded in a future tense. For example, "I know one day I will see how beautiful I truly am, inside and out" and "As I work through old past hurts and beliefs I know that I will be able to heal myself". Think of it as having a conversation about your future self, the person you are becoming. So, all the things you want this future person to be, their attitude and personality, you can use in your soothing positive self-talk. This is also a great technique to use to nourish your self-worth, "I am excited to see all of my hidden talents come to life" or something that recognizes your past behaviour and how you're changing, "I know that I haven't always been my own best friend but I am working on that and I am going to do my best going forward to show myself that I truly care and love who I am". Try to put as many sentences together as you can. You might find it easier to write it all down in the beginning so you get the hang of the correct words and tense to use.

Positive self-talk is a technique which helps you move your emotions up the emotional scale as outlined in chapter nine 'Your Emotional Shift'. When you talk positively with a sense of hope about what you're going through you should feel a sense of relief and a comfort from how the words make you feel. If you feel uncomfortable, pay attention because it means your feelings are guiding you to say a statement that offers greater relief. So all you have to do is make the statement less specific. Let how you feel be your guide as to how effective your self-talk is. There is no point in saying things that continue to make you feel uncomfortable. When you do this you shouldn't experience too much back chat from your mind.

I use positive self-talk when I am out walking. I just start talking about all the different areas in my life in a very positive way. I normally pick something that's been on my mind and I start off with "It's nice to be out walking today (this offers appreciation that I am exercising) Michael, what's happening with you?" I normally reply with something like: "I am feeling good today" or "I am feeling concerned or anxious or something else." And I continue to talk about what's going on in my life on a particular subject. It's an opportunity to not only get to the bottom of how I am feeling about something but also to talk my way into feeling more positive about the subject. Try it the next time you're out walking. Although don't do what I did and do it while walking in the city. I got quite a few looks!

Affirmations work similarly but have a different tone to them and because the tone is more definite they are more powerful in delivering the belief into your unconscious mind. The affirmation needs to be said in positive words and in the present tense about what you would like to achieve. You say it as you want it to be, not as it is right now or will be in the future. For example, "I love how my life is changing for the better", "My life keeps getting better and better every day", "Money is always available to me", "I have a wonderful new lover in my life", or "I am successful in everything I do". You get the idea! One of my favourite Louise Hay affirmations, which I learned many years ago and I still say to this day is, "All is well in my life. Everything is always working out for my highest good".

To really assist the rooting of your affirmations, you need to behave and evoke the emotional feelings as if you now have what you want. This is, of course, easier said than done. Remember it has to have the believability factor otherwise your mind will take much longer to accept it.

Your thoughts offer you the most amazing freedom of escaping your reality. You can picture things that may happen in the future and things that are not perceivable by you right now in your current situation, like imagining what your life would be like if you had all the money, love, friendship, family and work you needed to be happy, fulfilled and complete. However, your thoughts also work in contradiction to what you want for a better life and allow you to imagine the worse possible outcomes from the variety of situations that are going on in your life right now by creating fearful, worrisome feelings and outcomes.

When you picture a different life, with better opportunities, greater peace of mind, more financial support, you are actually doing a technique called mental rehearsal or visualization, which is the third of the three ways you can begin changing your internal story. Visualization, mental rehearsal is a positive way to use your imagination. It allows you to use mental imagery to become better, happier and more effective in everything you do and want to accomplish in your life. When you were a child you were an expert visualizer. Do you remember imagining being a Super Hero, a Princess or some other character that you became fascinated with? Visualization is used by millions of professional athletes to boost their strength, confidence and envisage a winning performance. For example, if you watch any short distance runner just before a race, you can see them using visualization to do a quick run through of certain aspects of their run in their mind.

Everyone from all walks of life, such as business executives, surgeons or musicians use imagery to prepare for all kinds of situations.

I take time every morning to visualize my day and things I want to experience in that day, week and month, and I visualize how I want my life to look and feel going forward. And all through images and my imagination.

How does it work? Well, you can experience real-world and imaginary actions in similar ways. Whether you walk ten miles or just picture it, you activate many of the same neural pathways that link your body and your mind. As mentioned already, and I don't mind repeating it because it is such an important bit of information to know, is that your unconscious mind does not know the difference between what is real and what is imagined. It didn't know when you were four, ten or fifteen years old and it doesn't know now, which is why you have so many dysfunctional beliefs operating in your mind.

Your unconscious mind will never disagree with you or believe you don't have something that you've imagined because your unconscious is your illogical, irrational, non-analytical mind and can't tell the difference between what is real and what is pretend. It will believe anything whether it makes logical sense or not. It only thinks in the present so believes what you're thinking and talking about is factual and happening right now. It's only your now fully mature conscious, thinking mind that is telling you to the contrary, and that's been taken from the belief system you have already built in your unconscious mind. It's a cycle you have to interrupt so that you can start to begin believing in what you want to achieve.

Getting Beyond What Is

Increasing the frequency of visualization work, positive self-talk, and affirmations might seem inconsequential small mental changes to make every day, but the more you do in favour of what you want to manifest and away from what you don't, will generate positive momentum and enable you to alter, modify and change many of your unconscious programmes and create a permanent mind shift. Good positive feedback thoughts mean that your work is having an impact, but if you're getting negative feedback don't be too worried, it just means that you still have some more work to do on that particular area of your life. Keep doing the work and before you know it the barriers will fall and you will begin taking opportunities that you wouldn't have considered before.

Remember the conversation you've been having with yourself has most likely been going on for many years, so adding new thought streams won't be accepted that easily. So as you begin to add new and more positive thoughts about something, they will initially meet with resistance. But persevere and they will take root and grow into the new beliefs that will support your new thoughts and thinking patterns. Affirmations are, of course, only part of the process. What you do for the rest of your day is vital to making any significant changes to your life.

I know it can be hard to change the conversation, especially when quite a lot of it is in your head. Thoughts manifest into many different things. They have a power like no other and when you read chapter thirteen 'The Law of Attraction' you will see even greater reasons to start changing your story about your thoughts. Thinking differently, even though you may not do it all the time in the beginning, will create a different perspective of the world for you. Put the right thoughts together and you will inspire and motivate yourself to do anything in your life.

" Positive thinking *doesn't mean you ignore difficult situations.* It means that you approach them in a way that is more **PRODUCTIVE** and **BENEFICIAL** to you. **"**

—Michael Nulty

CHAPTER TWELVE

What Are You Worth?

Nothing is more important than a healthy sense of self-worth. When you accept and embrace that you are a worthy person, life becomes simpler and lighter. You think and feel equal to everyone and everything. You appreciate that your abilities, thoughts and your emotions have value. You don't beat yourself up in difficult times or when you encounter setbacks. However, when you put your self down, make light of your talents and rubbish yourself in any way, you may think you're being humble, but what you think is modesty is actually an unconscious self-worth declaration.

Your level of self-worth today affects who you are and every single thing you do. It is what enables you to believe that you are capable of doing your best with your talents, contributing well to society, and deserving a fulfilling, happy and abundant life. However, one of the biggest obstacles to creating a new and better story is worthiness. In fact, many people unconsciously sabotage opportunities that come their way as they believe they are not worthy of them, or they aren't good enough to have them.

When your self-worth is healthy you trust your own judgement, you will make decisions based upon what you consider to be the best choice for you and your future, not what others think is best for you. You will believe in certain values and principles but capable of adjusting them if you need to do so. You're not stuck in the past worrying about what happened, nor are you continually looking into the future trying to predict what could happen. You learn from the past, plan for the future but live in the present. You have faith in your own ability to solve problems but when things go wrong, you can just as easily ask for help. You consider yourself to be equal not inferior or superior and accept even your limitations.

However, when your self-worth is low you give little value to your own opinions and ideas. You feel unworthy, incapable and incompetent in a lot of what you do. You are filled with doubts and criticism about your abilities and your identity. You can feel so poorly about yourself that the feelings keep you stuck in a permanent state of low self-worth, leading to attacks of anxiety or worry, even ending up with periods of depression.

Self-worth or self-esteem is something that can only come from within you. It is a judgement, an attitude towards your true self and your ego self. It's the sense of your own value or worth as a whole person, reflecting your own subjective emotional evaluation of the world you live in. You could say it's knowing that you are good, decent and great, without the need to show it off. You could as easily drive a brand new Mercedes car as confidently as you would drive a car that is perceived as old and rusty. You do things because you like them and how they feel to you, not because of what others might think of you which would be your ego presenting itself.

Your ego plays an important role in your life and also in your worth. It is the physical identity you present to the world, which has been constructed over time by you and made up of your worth, labels, masks, judgements, attitudes, memories, values and beliefs about yourself. You see yourself from a place of wholeness, warts and all, but the world only sees you through your ego, which is why other people see you very differently than you see yourself. People may see you as someone that's got it all together when inside you're just about holding it together. Your ego is built upon what other people say to you whereas your self-worth is built upon what you say to yourself.

Your ego will orient itself around the roles you play in your life both the professional ones and the personal ones. And as you identify with those roles more and more your ego wraps itself around. For example, "I am only an office worker", "I am only a housewife", "I am only a college drop out" and over time after telling yourself that you are only this and that, and less worthy than everyone by the words you use, you start to believe the roles you play are all you're capable of doing in your life.

Undervaluing your worth by attaching it to the roles you play works the other way, too. When you attach your worth to a career, financial earnings, titles and job prestige, you view your worth in terms of money, success and achievements. You become obsessed by having material objects and over time your perception shifts to value people by what they do rather than by who they are. But when you associate and equate your self-worth with doing something that is recognized by a monetary or socially discernible scale of prosperity and affluence, and then if you don't feel you meet that or you stop meeting those criteria due to a change in your circumstances, your self-worth can easily take a dive which sends you plummeting into depression.

If you want to know if you suffer a deficit of self-worth, answer this question "What would happen to my self-worth if everything I had spent years working for, my nice car, my clothes, my nice house, was taken away from me?"

We talk a lot about what we believe. We work on swapping our limiting beliefs and creating new beliefs. But we seldom take the time to consider our values and our value system as something that might also be restricting and hindering what we are trying to achieve in our life. Your values help you understand where and what your role in society is. They are a key motivator for everything you do, because if you don't value something it's likely you will ever put much effort into making it happen. Values emerge from a combination of your background, environment, experiences and an evolving sense of yourself. Some values stay with you throughout your life, while others develop and change as you do. They become the things against which you measure your choices, rationalize your behaviour and form as beliefs, which guide you on how to conduct your life in a way that is meaningful and satisfying for you.

Ask yourself these questions: "How do I show myself that I matter?" "Do I deserve to have what I desire?" "Is my new and better story something I truly value?" Take note of your answers as they give you a great place to begin restoring your self-worth.

We all wear a mask at some stage of our lives to hide who we are because, at times it's easier to be someone different in order to fit into an certain environment and situation in society. But if you're truly honest with yourself, you can never hide from how you see yourself, regardless of what ego version of you, you show to the outside world or where in the world you take yourself.

Finding yourself and becoming aligned with who you really are is probably the most profound and life changing experience that you will ever encounter. It is the ultimate goal in life and when you find the way to connect with your own true self, your life takes on a different meaning. However, when you disconnect yourself from who you truly are in preference of the personality that society has caused you to portray, you live a life of separation from all that you have the potential to become.

Bringing your self-worth back to a healthy state, believing you are worthy of all that you strive to achieve and creating a new and better story can be challenging when you have spent years belittling yourself and taking on board unconsciously negative comments, expectations and attitudes of others. However, because your self-worth is something that can only be rebuilt by you, you can correct what you say, what you think and learn to value yourself again.

Positive self-talk, affirming your self-worth to yourself, can be a very good way to start changing the internal negative dialogue that you may have going on inside your head. Dedicate a set time during your day to declare and affirm to yourself that you're a great person, you're special, you're wonderful, you're lovable and you're loved. If you can do your affirming work in front of a mirror you will get greater results. But it can be hard to face yourself and change the conversation from "You're ugly", You're no good", "I don't like you", to nicer, kinder and more compassionate words. The same rules apply that I outlined in chapter eleven 'Positive Changes' about affirmations and the believable factor.

If affirmations were magical it would be very easy to build self-worth and to change and create beliefs! The reality is somewhat different, and while it's vital to use positive self-talk and affirmations to build new sets of pathways in your unconscious mind, they are part of the solution. It's important for you to act on your sense of self-worth by recognizing and accepting responsibility, owning up to the fact that you are in control of your attitude, your reactions and your sense of worth. The root of poor self-worth is really letting other people and circumstances serve as the source of lowering your self-worth.

So, where possible avoid hanging out and listening to negative people who have low self-worth. People who regret their choices in life, but who are very quick to inflict their distress and negativity for a life they didn't live, upon you. Instead, find and listen to people with healthy self-worth, who are willing and happy to share their insights and learnings with you, and will be willing to guide you around the twists and turns of life.

Your story can easily become defined and set by other people's expectations: what job you choose, where to reside, who you date, who you become friends with. So don't lose your own identity and the person you truly are by trying to live up to an image or an idea of what you think your friends, family and co-workers want you to be. When other people praise you and say nice things to you, it is your ego self that basks in the compliment, but it doesn't affect your self-worth because that's waiting for your compliment.

When you stop trying to please everyone else, what you want in your life will rise to the surface, and you can start working on your own happiness, love and self-worth. As you change your focus from other people back to your own self you may find that some people in your present life won't like that you're doing your own thing, and that's fine. If we all did the same thing, the world wouldn't get very far. Let you do you first, and then you can get around to helping other people out with their happiness and love.

Treating yourself as you would your best friend and coming to love all that you are, the person you were, are and will be is the greatest gift you can give yourself. Loving your self is not expressed through preening oneself all day and constantly announcing how great you are, as that is actually insecurity. Loving your self is about treating yourself with the same care, tolerance, generosity, and compassion as you would treat a special friend, free from judgement and criticism. Remember, only you can give yourself the esteem boost you need, as no one else is living your life, but you.

"Don't be afraid to be different.
What you see as difference is
UNIQUENESS &
INDIVIDUALITY.
Embrace your diversity
and *let yourself shine.* "

—Michael Nulty

CHAPTER THIRTEEN

The Law of Attraction

You may have already come across or read about the Law of Attraction as in 2006, the concept of the Law of Attraction gained a lot of renewed exposure with the release of the film *The Secret*, followed by the book later that year. The movie and book gained widespread attention in all the media. All the top chat shows including *Larry King Live*, *The Oprah Winfrey Show* and many other shows brought a law which was only known and practised by some to the masses around the world. Millions of people began practising the principle of the law, 'like attracts like' which sums up the idea that we attract whatever we desire or expect into our life experience that which we want and that which we don't want.

So, millions of people all over the world started to use and practise the law to bring them all the things they desired in their lives, new cars, new jobs, new lovers, more money, you name it people asked for it. Some received what they asked for, others had to settle for disappointment when things didn't quite show up as they had thought and hoped. They were missing the real secret: believing it can happen and allowing it to happen. You attract into your reality things, situations, even struggles that correspond with your dominant thoughts, emotions and beliefs both conscious and unconscious about those things, situations and struggles.

The simplest way to understand it is to think about everything being two subjects: the Lack of something and the Abundance of the same thing. You desire something because you don't have it or you don't have enough of it (Lack) and you would like to have lots more of it (Abundance). So you declare to the universe: "I want more of X and Y." But the universe doesn't hear those words, it hears what those words mean to you in the form of what you believe, what you think and how you feel about the subject X and Y. And the Law of Attraction brings to you only that which you offer as your dominant intention through the language of the universe, vibration.

Let's take money for example, which coincidentally was one of the first things I asked for when I came across the Law of Attraction in the 1990s. So, you declare very much in the same tone and tense as affirmations "I want more money". But when you talk about your money situation you bring into the conversation your emotions – are you anxious and worried about the bills you have right now, do you hate having to pay your bills or have you a limiting belief that says "you never have enough money". At the time that was my dominant vibration. And so the undertone of your request is not about having lots of money (Abundance) it's about the fact that you don't have enough money (Lack). And so under those conditions the Law of Attraction can only respond with more of the same.

So, don't think for one second that the Law of Attraction dishes out punishment or acts as judge and jury on whether you do or do not deserve what you're asking for. That's all you and what you've got going on inside your head. It is mostly your ego self that asks for stuff which is the same for everyone. You see the neighbours with a nice new car and you think I'd like a nice new car too. But it is your own self-worth and beliefs along with that voice in your head saying "This won't happen, because nothing good ever happens to me" that puts a spanner in the works.

You make the mistake when you assume that because you are saying the words, maybe even being positive and smiling as you say them that the Law of Attraction is receiving your message in the same way. When you desire something and think, feel and believe something different consciously and unconsciously, you disallow what you want to receive. When you don't believe it for whatever reason, you will not receive it for those same reasons, but instead, you'll receive what you do believe about it.

To help you understand a little better how something in the great big universe can affect your life on a day to day basis, I have to take you back to class and give you a quick science lesson. Our experience tells us that our reality is made up of physical material things. But what we perceive as our physical material world is not physical or material, it's energy. Scientists back as far as Plato who was a philosopher in the third century BC, to Albert Einstein in the twentieth century who developed the Theory of Relativity, to the quantum physicists of today who are continuously discovering more and more about life and the most astonishing things about our planet and the universe. They know already that everything in the universe is made up of energy, our houses, our cars, our phones, the trees, animals and everything we interact with is a form of energy vibrating at different rates and frequencies, in different forms and shapes, constantly at flow and changing all the time. We are so much more than flesh and bone. We are really beings of energy, radiating our own unique energy signature and translating our environment into the physical equivalent.

In our physical environment, we have become accustomed to translating vibration into meaning for ourselves without ever really consciously knowing it's happening. What we see with our eyes and hear with our ears is a physical interpretation of vibration. For example, our radio, telephone and television airwaves all translate vibration into things that our physical senses understand. A dog can hear a dog whistle when it has been blown but our human ears cannot detect it. We have come to accept these things in society as fact and our reality, without ever breaking down or even understanding completely how they work. They all just happen and we accept them that way.

The Law of Attraction

So, you have your physical manifested reality which you see, hear, touch, taste and smell. But then you also have what is called a vibrational reality where your wants and desires are born and as the energy and the vibration is transmitted to the universe, the powerful Law of Attraction responds accordingly and those wants and desires begin to manifest into their physical equivalent in your reality.

My purpose in explaining vibration and energy a little is to give you some context as to how the Law of Attraction works. The more sense something makes even vaguely, the more your mind will work to bring further meaning to it. However, if you can't grasp it right now, don't get hung up on trying to force it. I still find it hard to wrap my head around a lot of quantum physics stuff, too. All you really need to know is that everything in the universe is communicating, reacting, responding and interacting through the universal language of vibration which is your thoughts, your emotions, your feelings and your beliefs. The Law of Attraction works whether you believe it or not.

If this is the first time you're hearing about the Law of Attraction you may be surprised to know that it has been in existence for quite a long time, but only since the nineteenth century has the term 'Law of Attraction' been used. New Thought authors at the time, Prentice Mulford and Ralph Trine wrote about the Law of Attraction and its principle, like attracts like. Ralph Trine wrote in his book, *In Tune With The Infinite* in 1897: "The law of attraction works universally on every plane of action, and we attract whatever we desire or expect. If we desire one thing and expect another, we become like houses divided against themselves, which are quickly brought to desolation. Determine resolutely to expect only what you want, then you will attract only what you wish for." Charles Haanel, author of *The Master Key System*, wrote in 1912: "The law of attraction will certainly and unerringly bring to you the conditions, environment and experiences in life, corresponding with your habitual, characteristic, predominant mental attitude."

The last one hundred years has seen a surge in interest in the possibility of any person being able to attract conditions and experiences that they predominantly think about or which they desire or expect. I think that two of the most influential books on the subject are *Think and Grow Rich* (1937) by Napoleon Hill and *You Can Heal Your Life* (1984) by Louise Hay. I would highly recommend you read either or both of these books. I read both when I was in my late twenties and they helped me break down so many barriers and allowed me to believe in myself and what I could do in the world with my thoughts, beliefs and harnessing the Law of Attraction.

Today, the foremost authority on the Law of Attraction and the greatest teacher of all is Abraham-Hicks and I would highly recommend you read any material from Abraham. You can check out contact information in my acknowledgment section at the beginning of the book. I truly believe that the more you know and come to understand about the Law of Attraction, the more you come to appreciate the power of the universe and the power of you, to create your life as you would like it to be.

The Law of Attraction

The basic foundation to the Law of Attraction is that energies that are alike are attracted to each other. Energy is constantly vibrating, and the objects we perceive as solid are actually just energy vibrating at a particular frequency. Energy vibrates at different speeds which cause different frequencies or wavelengths and these waves of energy are attracted to other waves just like themselves, or in other words one frequency attracts another that is the same wavelength as itself. Everything is here and now, in various states of visibility and invisibility depending upon the frequency you are tuned to. Think of it like tuning into a radio station. You know that there are lots of different stations out there but only when you turn your radio dial to the same frequency and wavelength of your favourite radio station can you hear what's going on.

You are continually influenced by the Law of Attraction. Every belief you hold has been strengthened through the Law of Attraction. And it is all happening right now, whether you're aware of it, believe in its existence or not. Your most influential frequency or wavelength is determined by your mental attitude to your now reality, your habitual thoughts, beliefs, emotions and feelings. A positive mental attitude to your life attracts to you positive experiences, circumstances and conditions. While a negative mental attitude attracts conditions that you perceive as negative and unwanted to your reality.

Everything that you are paying attention to, giving your focus or concentrated thought to, physical and imagined, you offer and include as your own vibration. Whether you are judging the wrongness and rightness of what's happened to you or to others, playing negative 'what if' scenarios over and over again, responding to struggles in a defeatist way or complaining about conditions, because they are not the way you need them to be. All of it is included in your vibration and the Law of Attraction interprets and accepts it as your dominant intent and reflects back to you unbiasedly more of the same.

The Law of Attraction simply performs as an orchestrator to bring like energies together. You could consider the Law of Attraction to be the ultimate courier, working every moment of every day and you, the sender and the recipient of every possible object, situation and circumstance. Nothing is ever too small or too big to be handled and brought to you by the Law of Attraction. It delivers exactly what you send to it, all of that which you think, say, believe and feel about a lot. If you are unclear as to what you require and give mixed information you will find that receiving what you want is difficult. But if you are clear and resolute in what you are sending, then trust and expect that everything will be delivered to you. You will receive all that you want and desire.

What can cause a lot of people to struggle with using the Law of Attraction is trying to figure out how it will happen. We think if we can somehow figure out how it's going to happen we can believe it's going to. It doesn't work that way, because we have to believe it before we can see it. If we have to see it before we believe it, well what we're looking for will always evade us. As a generation of people, we have become accustomed to trusting what we see and know, but not so much trusting in what is unseen and unknown. I have come to experience that everything is essentially here and now, in various states of visibility and invisibility with our mind constructing the reality we perceive. There is no such thing as the unknown, only things that are temporarily hidden from us.

Other aspects of the Law of Attraction that trip people up is that they think that if they ask for a pile of money that somehow when they check their bank account that more zeros will have been added to their bank balance in a matter of days. The manifestations come in many different forms and they don't happen instantly. It may be a thought, an idea pops into your head about something. You receive an impulse to do something or go somewhere. You begin to feel better about something that you have been worried about. When you open your mind to believing that something is possible the opportunities will show up in your experience, not because you deserve them but because it's the law.

Remember a simple thing like a thought is actually a manifestation. Everything is lining up for you so don't wait for the physical to just appear out of the sky. Become consciously and cognitively aware of the signs of early manifestation, follow the trail it provides for you and I promise you, you will be amazed at what happens.

I suggest you start off with simple things. Things that don't have such an emotional undercurrent as money and relationships. The idea is to become familiar with asking and allowing what you've asked for to manifest. When I realized more money wasn't coming as quickly as I thought back in the late 1990s, mostly because of old beliefs about money, I became very frustrated. Until one day I decided that I was going to just practise the law and learn how to manifest things. And that is the key, practice and patience So I decided that I was going to ask to receive things that had no significant meaning to me other than I like them, but more importantly, I hadn't any back issues with the subject matter like I had with money.

So for one month I practised trying to receive colours. Every day I would choose a different colour to see in my reality, some days I punched it up a couple of notches and asked for three or four colours together and I was amazed. One day actually blew my mind away, I had chosen the colour green and I thought to myself, that maybe I should have chosen a different colour because all the plants and trees where I lived were obviously green, but nevertheless I continued with the green theme. That afternoon I needed to drive to a store in a nearby town and on the way there and out of nowhere I took a wrong turn, and ended up driving down a street painted green. I had to get out of the car and touch the street because I thought I was seeing things. What was even more amazing was that I had been on that street before and I had never noticed it was painted green. But the universe through the Law of Attraction orchestrated what I called my rendezvous with the green road.

I continued practising the law with small things until I worked through much of my own back story and there was a lot to be sorted. But as I started to work out the bigger picture of my life – what

I wanted my life to be, what role I wanted to play – my intentions became clearer, my beliefs became stronger and my resistance faded. Job opportunities came flooding in, promotions in those jobs came, great salaries came with those jobs. I thrived for many years as a leader in business going from one success to another, collecting awards for my work across many industries and it can be the same for you.

You do not have to learn how to apply the Law of Attraction, because it does all the work and it is already operating in your life perfectly, whether you accept it or not. Your only work is to bring up to speed what you think, what you say, what you believe and how you feel about what you want for your life. Acknowledge and accept that the circumstances of your physical world have a deep rooted connection to that of your inner world and are brought together by the powerful Law of Attraction.

Amazing things start to happen when you keep on going without continually judging your progress. The universe through the Law of Attraction responds to you because you demonstrate willpower that says you're not going to give up. There is nothing more uplifting and motivating than the universe through the Law of Attraction conspiring with you to achieve your dreams.

Your life is a journey and is continually shifting and moving with every new experience, knowledge and belief gained. Your life expands through your natural wants and desire for more, and you experience life through the contrast of what you have and what you would like. You create when you notice or observe something, either pleasing or unpleasing and focus upon it for a period of time, causing it to be included in your vibrational offering. And it turns from a thought into a physical manifestation in your reality over time. Nothing remains exactly the same although it may seem that way when you are going through difficult times.

To experience profound transformation in any area of your life, you must first become the master of your own mind. When you create a fertile growing place, you will discover that the seed of your desire is all that is necessary for it to blossom into something greater. The only real work needed is on yourself.

" Don't get discouraged by what's *not happening*. Look around you and notice the things that *are*. You'll be IMPRESSED by what you've ACHIEVED. **"**

—Michael Nulty

CHAPTER FOURTEEN

Conditional Dependency

So many people today live their life conditionally and dependent on situations, circumstances and even people being a certain way in order to feel good and to be happy. And when the conditions are not the way they are supposed to be the ability to feel good or feel better becomes a struggle. Conditions can add immense joy and contentment to your life but can also do the exact opposite. When you give power to something outside yourself to affect and even control how you feel, you open yourself up to the possibility of a state of dependency, which will keep you separated from ever really enjoying and appreciating living your life unconditionally.

Your present reality is full of conditions from every day stuff, like traffic, commerce, weather, knowledge and emotions, to more influential conditions, like money, love, health, work and family, which probably started as mere every day stuff but have now become key factors in allowing you to feel good and feel happy in your life. You may even have become somewhat reliant and dependent on these conditions from old thought patterns, beliefs and information about the role the conditions play in your reality.

So, it's worth taking a moment to consider how much of feeling good and being happy in your life is dependent on situations, circumstances, even people being a certain way in order for your life to feel good to you. Conditional happiness is dependent on external factors, having pleasurable experiences the likes of going on holidays, having a party, shopping and other things you like to do. Or from that buzz you get when everything in your life is going well. Unconditional or authentic happiness is not dependent on anything outside you. It is the simple joy of being that comes from within you.

However, you will notice that feeling good, free or happy fades and is even placed on hold when certain conditions are not the way you would like them to be or the way you believe they should be in order for you to feel good. You subscribe to the belief that "I will be happy when … happens". And as you wait on the external events to become a reality, your happiness is postponed to a future time while you live in a state of 'becoming' happy and not being happy in the present here and now. And so you get caught up in the endless chase of pleasurable experiences and suppress all those experiences that are uncomfortable.

Money, love, health, work, family and friends are conditions that can place a strong grasp on how you feel and even cause you to become consumed by them through your continuous focus and attention upon them. But the struggle and battle is not because of the actual condition, it is due to your focus upon the absence, lack or status of the condition or conditions compared with where you believe they should be in order for your life to feel better and for you to feel good about yourself.

Your constant focus upon the lack, status and absence of certain conditions mostly generates the feelings of doubt, worry, anxiety and fear. You may find that even when the conditions are the way you want them to be, the emotions of doubt, worry, anxiety and fear are lingering in the background because you have developed a specific thinking pattern and belief about the conditions which is hard to change. A belief that happiness is dependent and can fade causes the times when you are happy to be slightly tainted with a certain amount of anxiety and fear of it all going away.

During my earlier years, unknowingly I developed a strong limiting belief that convinced me every day for years that if I could make conditions a certain way and keep them that way my life and my capacity to feel good and be happy would dramatically change. And although money, love, good health, a successful career, loving family and friends did definitely make me feel better and bring great happiness into my life, it always felt temporary because it was conditional living and not living unconditionally.

Your success, happiness or anything else you need and really desire is not dependent on anything other than you. However, to be happy and fulfilled in your present reality, you have got to stop judging the rightness and wrongness of conditions, even wrestling them to the ground. Stop treating and trying to change the condition to make it better. Every time you think or talk about the condition you breathe greater life into it and the Law of Attraction brings you more of the same. Nothing you do can change any condition that has physically manifested into your reality because it's happening, it's already manifested. But it only exists as a temporary element of your present reality for now. The condition will eventually change, which could be in minutes, hours, days, weeks or years, depending on how willing you are to release the condition and empower yourself or hold onto the condition and remain disempowered by continuing your attention upon it which reinforces your dependency.

A dependent condition begins life as an aspect of circumstance but it is interpreted as an annoyance and frustration in your life. And although you may have a deep rooted past belief about the condition which needs to be addressed, your conscious mind only senses how it is affecting your life in its present state and how your good feelings are altered when the condition is and isn't a certain way. As you put more and more effort into improving the condition you slowly become addicted and obsessed with trying to change it – change your money situation, find your love/relationship, lose the weight and so on. All it seems to make more of though are periods of stress, long periods of anxiety and even depression for a time.

But you don't have to put your life on hold waiting on conditions to be a certain way and you don't have to disempower yourself by giving control to something outside yourself to influence how you feel about your present reality or indeed your life. There is a way to feel good and be happy unconditionally. You just need to change your own personal relationship with the condition and in time you will understand why it is the way it is – it is a deep rooted belief or it has been your constant focus and thinking about the condition that has created the dependency.

The real secret which many people don't realize is that although you can't change the condition you do have the ability to change the way you feel about it. When you begin to change how you feel about the condition, the condition loses its power to influence how you feel about it and you take back control over the conditions in your life. So let me give you an example. I will continue the money theme as it continues the money theme from chapter thirteen 'The Law of Attraction'. You have a condition that when you have money you feel good but when you have no money life can be a struggle, because then you're worried about having no money, maybe not being able to pay bills, put food on the table etc. So you put your effort into trying to make more money, but nothing seems to change. In fact, it only seems to get worse. The condition has now formed into a belief about your lack of money, and the Law of Attraction responds with more thoughts, feelings and further evidence that support that belief.

When a condition that you have becomes dependent upon the centre of your reality and your vibration is fixed upon the struggle and why it isn't the way it should be, you sacrifice your own personal happiness and good feelings, and the continued emphasis can be destructive, crippling emotionally and mentally. If you cannot find happiness in where you are now, your happiness is perpetually on hold depending on a condition that does not exist yet, and you will discover that you will always only be temporarily happy but never truly happy. Being happy is a choice and it must be unconditional. Be present in this moment and do what makes you feel good because what is most important is how you feel in relation to what you want. Your power is over your mind not outside events.

The only way you can reverse situations that are conditional is to change the story you're telling about the condition. The more you alter how you feel about the condition using soothing positive self-talk the more you will let go of the struggle and stop trying to change the condition and start trying to change yourself. You get to choose how you react to each and every situation that comes into your life. You can see your life as ordinary, burdensome and become weighed down with the problems and challenges of living each day. Or you can expand your vision and see obstacles as an opportunity to respond with a new and different perspective. When you change how you feel, the condition miraculously changes. When you learn to live your life with conditions and around those conditions being the way they are, you empower yourself to be a deliberate creator and the author of your own life story.

" It takes COURAGE
to do the things you fear
the most. When you
CHALLENGE your
fear you open your life to so
much more than you ever
imagined. **"**

—Michael Nulty

CHAPTER FIFTEEN

Creating New Beliefs

Changing your beliefs about something allows possibilities to exist where they didn't before, which in turn not only changes your behaviour and emotions but also how you go about living your life. Some of the things I believe now I would not have believed five years ago. But through my willingness to open my mind and relax about what I did believe, I've been able to change many things in my life for the better.

You have beliefs about everything in your life but not all beliefs are limiting your success, so it's your work to discover the beliefs that support the new changes and the ones that don't support the new better chapter you're looking to create. One set of beliefs will allow you to move forward, the other will offer resistance and compelling reasons to stay the way you are even if it is in a life of misery.

Ask yourself what do you believe about yourself; do you think that you are not educated enough, maybe you feel you're not good enough or maybe you think it's selfish to want more than you already have? All are limiting you in some way. What do you believe about work? Do you think work is supposed to be difficult, that it requires sacrifices or maybe you believe like me that to be successful you have to give up your personal life for your work? Probably the area where limiting beliefs are most evident for all of mankind is on the subject of money. Do you know what your true beliefs are about money? Is it that there is never enough money? This was one of mine because it also supported that I wasn't enough. Maybe it's that nice people don't have money, or people who have money are not nice. Or maybe it's only rich people have money and that everyone else has to struggle. Whatever you believe, you believe, but it is so important to recognize that beliefs are not facts, and they may only be true to you.

To help you work through your limiting beliefs I have come up with a four step recipe that will successfully enable you to modify and change the limiting beliefs operating in your mind. The four steps are: Identify, Confront, Dispute and Exchange. For the mental work to be effective you need to physically put your words to paper. This is a process and keeping track and following through from identifying a belief to neutralizing and repeating it will decide whether you change the limiting belief or not. Writing down everything will allow you to think better, learn more and remember more. You won't get distracted quite as easily and it frees up your conscious mind's mental RAM, remember you can only process up to seven chunks of information at any one time.

Although you may be tempted to try to conquer many beliefs across different subject matters simultaneously, you will get the best results if you work on one subject matter whether that is money, work, relationship or self-worth and the core limiting beliefs associated with that subject. I would suggest you start with a subject matter that you feel you have some limiting beliefs about that are most likely false now and ones you think you can have a quick impact on. It's important for your own self-confidence that you see results sooner rather than later, which wouldn't be the case with deep rooted limited beliefs.

Over time beliefs become part of a web of beliefs, so when you start changing one the others rise up with resistance to that change. It's the biggest reason why so many people give up trying to change their beliefs and instead lower their expectations to align with what they do believe. The beliefs you're trying to change have been with you for a long time and unknowingly you probably continue to breathe life into them every day. It doesn't mean that you can't change them, it means that you have to approach them with intelligence, understanding and knowledge about how they were made in the first place and how your mind operates. You can move on to changing deeper beliefs as you start to build confidence in your own ability to change your limiting beliefs.

You are about to change your life so it's worth putting great effort into the exercise. Set some time aside in your diary every day to go through the process. Prepare yourself to answer some very probing and difficult questions. Get a new pad, one that feels good to touch and a pen that writes nicely on the page.

You need to be as open and as honest as you have ever been with yourself before. The process must be done in step order – it's not a pick and mix, you can't skip a step because it's too hard. You start by establishing what your limiting beliefs are.

STEP 1: IDENTIFY

You begin by identifying and writing down your top four beliefs or thoughts that are limiting what you are doing or not doing in your life on a specific subject. What ever subject you decide to begin with make the heading 'My Beliefs About X'. But how do you know if a belief is limiting, sabotaging and producing negative consequences in your life? Here are some suggestions on how to begin identifying limiting beliefs.

► Look at the things on this subject you've put considerable amount of effort into changing and even though you've tried and tried you continue to struggle to make the situation the way you want it to be. It's most likely you are operating a limiting belief.
► Write down the things that you have come to believe about this subject. You are really only interested in the beliefs that are holding you back. Notice how you feel about each belief as you

write them down. The ones that make you feel uncomfortable are most likely limiting you in some way.

► Pay attention to your thoughts; thoughts which drag you down, trigger emotionally negative feelings and make you think the opposite of what you want your life to be now. Limiting beliefs are usually the same thoughts that replay in your mind every day over and over, or the familiar thoughts that are triggered in specific scenarios, like when you think about money, work or your own self.

STEP 2: CONFRONT

This step is about calling out the beliefs you identified in step one. But coming face to face with them is not an easy task, so take your time to truly confront each belief. Ask yourself why you believe this. Confronting your beliefs is about understanding them, not challenging them at this stage. Move to a new page in your pad and put the heading 'What I Know About Belief X'. You should write this heading for each of the four beliefs you've identified in step one. Think of it as a fact finding and recovery mission working to the following guidelines.

► Reflect upon your past and present life, and write down instances and experiences when the belief has manifested and when it is reinforced.

▶ Take the time to properly explore the belief. You are trying to see if you can trace back the belief to a time in your life when it first emerged.

▶ Write down all the answers that come up regardless of whether you think they're relevant or not. Don't judge or criticize anything that comes to mind. Remember you're trying to uncover the real truth about the belief.

▶ If you feel you're not good enough, ask yourself the question: "Good enough for what?"

STEP 3: DISPUTE

Because beliefs are built upon a mix of fact and fictitious statements, once you understand more about why you believe what you believe, you can dispute them and cast a shadow of doubt over them. Many beliefs are formed during the critical and early formative years of your life and follow you from your childhood into adulthood as you continue to reinforce them even if they are not true now.

If the same things were said to you now as an adult you would discredit the source and the information would get dismissed as not credible or ridiculous. Think of yourself as a prosecuting lawyer, looking for incriminating evidence that proves your belief is guilty of taking away possibilities and your freedom to choose. Create a new heading 'What Is Not True About Belief X'. As in step two, you will have a similar heading for each of the four limiting beliefs. Using what you have learned and understand now about each of the four limiting beliefs you will begin disputing their accuracy and truth.

▶ Gather information about the belief that would suggest that it is not the truth now that you once thought it was. For example, on the belief mentioned earlier 'Only rich people have money and everyone else has to struggle'. This belief is only a fiction as many people who were born into poverty have become billionaires; you only have to look at Oprah Winfrey or Louise Hay to see this. But you can look closer at your own life, other family members and your friends to see if this belief is true and believable now.

▶ Make a list of your own personal qualities, such as your intelligence, skills, mental abilities, your positive attitude or your willingness to change and extend your frame of knowledge. If you are suffering with low self-worth don't allow your feelings to cloud the actual facts. I have no doubt that you have a lot to lay claim to. Make sure you put them all down even if you don't believe that you have achieved much.

▶ Make a second list of your external resources: a loving, supportive family, years of work experience, education or physical abilities. Things you have already acquired or have already achieved. Be aware of your ego playing its role in offering embellishments. The list must be truly factual, not overstated through ego or understated by your self-worth.

STEP 4: EXCHANGE

Step four is about counteracting an existing limiting belief by creating a new belief that is either true for your life now or a statement you want to be true. Your old beliefs won't fade away or disappear unless you do something to force them into retirement. In the beginning your mind will reject most things that you don't already believe unconsciously. When you make a new statement like "I am beautiful" or "I have lots of money", your mind will tell you that it's not true because that is the story you have stored in your unconscious mind about your appearance, self-worth and your financial situation. However, if you have been able to understand the limiting beliefs and where they come from, and been able to offer some evidence to support that they may not be true, the resistance you feel will be less than if you haven't done steps two and three. The heading for step four is 'What Do I Want To Believe Now About X'. To begin exchanging your limiting beliefs you must do the following work.

► Firstly, you must come up with your new belief statements that you want to replace your current limiting beliefs; statements that support you and what you want for your new life now and in the future. For example, "I am not good enough" is changed by saying "I am good enough just as I am". "There is never enough money", is changed by saying "I always have more than enough money to use, spare and share". Take some time to craft the statement

162

correctly as you're creating new beliefs that will transform your life.

▶ Secondly, become aware of what you're thinking as much as you can and whenever you catch yourself thinking an old limiting belief immediately exchange it by repeating your new belief statement. Even if it feels awkward just keep adding the new belief after the old one pops into your head.

The above two actions begin the neutralizing process and allow you to begin exchanging one belief for another, but they will need further help to change your core beliefs by using positive self-talk, affirmations and visualization. Positive self-talk, affirmations, and visualization are the key to helping you start changing the internal and external negative dialogue that you have going on inside your head.

▶ Soothing positive self-talk is about making a series of soft positive statements. They are worded in a future tense and tend to be more general than affirmations offering less resistance to your mind. For example, "I know one day I will see how beautiful I truly am, inside and out" and "As I open my mind to new possibilities I can see now that money can enter my life in so many different ways". Think of it as having a conversation about your future self – the person you are becoming. So, all the things you want this future person to be, their attitude and personality you can use in your soothing positive self-talk. This is also a great technique to use to nourish your self-worth "I am excited to see all of my hidden talents come to life", or something that recognizes your past behaviour and how you're changing, "I know that I haven't always been my own best friend but I am working on that and I am going to do my best going forward to show myself that I truly care about and love who I am".

▶ Affirmations have a different tone to them and because the tone is more definite they are more powerful in delivering the belief into your unconscious mind. Neuroscience now proves that thoughts can change the structure of our brain and affirmations when practised deliberately and repeatedly reinforce the chemical pathways in your mind strengthening neural connections. For the affirmations to be effective they need to be said in positive words and in the present tense about what you would like to achieve. You say it as you want it to be, not as it is right now or will be in the future. For example, "I love how my life is changing for the better", "My life keeps getting better and better every day", "Money is always available to me", "I have a wonderful new lover in my life", or "I am successful in everything I do". Use the same exchanging belief statements as affirmations. To really assist the rooting of your affirmations, you need to behave and evoke the emotional feelings as if you now have what you want. Which, is of course easier said than done. Remember it has to have the believability factor otherwise your mind will take much longer to accept it. An affirmation is a beginning point. It opens the way. You are saying to your unconscious mind: "I am taking responsibility. I am aware there is something I can do to change." If you continue to say the affirmation, either you will be ready to let whatever it is go and the affirmation will come true, or it will open a new avenue to you. You may get a brilliant brainstorm, or a friend may call you and ask, "Have you ever tried this?" You will be led to the next step that will help you make the changes you want.

▶ Visualization or mental rehearsal is about transforming your inner world which leads to the realization of results in your outer world. Within your inner world you can do anything and be anyone you choose, no matter what's happening in your external life. As you have heard me say a few times now, "nothing changes on the outside, until it changes on the inside first". Visualization is a conscious proactive activity where you actively imagine things in a specific way in order to positively impact your life. It allows you to use mental imagery and emotions to perform a mental rehearsal. When you picture a different life, with better opportunities, greater peace of mind, more financial support, you are actually doing what is called 'visualization'. Whether you walk ten miles or just picture it, you activate many of the same neural pathways that link your body and your mind. While you are visualizing, your conscious mind is aware that what you are doing isn't real and pretend, and it's just a creation of your imagination, like dreaming while awake. But as you have discovered in chapter six 'One Mind, Two Sets Of Rules', your unconscious mind is only present in the here and now, and believes that what you're thinking and talking about is factual and happening right now, because remarkably your unconscious mind doesn't distinguish the difference between what you think is real and what you imagine is real. It takes it all as real. Visualization is quite simple but doing it properly takes preparation and practice. Before you begin visualizing you need to:

▷ Identify the subject you're going to work on first. Are you going to visualize more money, a new love or some other scenario?

▷ Next you need to decide the individual scenarios of your life with more money, a new lover or another situation. For example, if you are looking for more money, is your scenario about living in a beautiful new fully furnished house, driving your new top of the range car or receiving a promotion at work?

▷ Writing the different scenarios down will help you focus and allow you to visualize with greater clarity. You don't need to write every detail as your imagination will create the finer details. It's about creating a framework for your mind so that you keep your visualizing focused and on what you want to achieve.

▷ Practise with different scenarios to see which ones make you feel the best. You visualize it as you want it to be, not as it is right now or will be in the future. The same way you repeat affirmations.

▷ Set aside five minutes a day when you are most relaxed either after you wake up in the morning, before you go to bed or after meditation. Sit in a comfortable position or you can lie down, and close your eyes. Start to think about the specific scenario that you'd like to visualize for this session. Create this new situation in your mind as vividly and with as much detail as you can. Visualize yourself achieving what you're aspiring for, see yourself doing the activity, see how good you are at it, how it feels to you. And finally, recreate in your body and mind the feelings you think you would be experiencing as you engage in this activity. You now have manifested the outcome to something you truly desire, so you should feel excited and happy. Once you feel your five minutes are up, open your eyes now and resume your day. Make this part of your daily routine and you will be amazed at how much improvement you will see you in your life.

Once you have completed the first round of four steps, it's worth revisiting each step again on the same subjects. You will discover a lot more information can come up the second time round that you couldn't think of the first time. Once you start the process it's just a matter of repeating it across all your core limiting beliefs. One of the biggest reasons why we don't reach the goals we set is not our lack of intelligence, experience or motivation it is because we don't practise enough. Persevere and your new beliefs will take root and grow invisibly and unconsciously into the new beliefs that will support your new thoughts and thinking pattern and your new life.

I believe that if you have been given a dream to be, have or do something, then you already have everything you need within you to achieve that dream. You already have the skills, talents and abilities you need, you just don't know it yet. So don't hold yourself back by thinking and feeling that you need to be more ready than you are now, that you need to know more, take one more course, do one more thing before you go for your dream.

You can achieve success if you are committed to what you want, believe you can achieve it and adopt a can do positive attitude in spite of the challenges you're going through.

" Holding on to a past life that doesn't serve you any more prevents a better one coming forward. LET GO, MOVE ON and EMBRACE a *brighter future.* **"**

—Michael Nulty

CHAPTER SIXTEEN

Boosting Your Self-Worth

Self-worth is a belief system that you create as you grow and evolve through your life. It is interchangeable with self-confidence, self-belief and self-love. Although some people may portray themselves as outgoing and confident, it doesn't necessarily mean that they have an abundance of self-worth. Certain situations that happen to you at an early age have an effect on how you feel about yourself and your perception of who you are. Comments people say to you, the experiences you have, the struggles you go through and the lessons you learn all impact on your self-worth and what you believe about who you are.

One of the greatest challenges we face in changing our life is believing we are enough. We are held to a belief, an old memory, fear and early childhood conditioning that tells us unconsciously that we are not enough and so we live out a life missing opportunities, not taking the jobs we want, not attracting the relationships we need because we don't feel worthy of great things.

Bringing your self-worth back to a healthy state and believing you are worthy of all that you strive to achieve and creating a new and better story can be challenging when you have spent years belittling yourself and unconsciously taking on board negative comments, expectations and attitudes of others. However, because your self-worth is something that can be rebuilt by you, you can correct what you say, what you think and learn to value yourself again.

Self-worth has nothing to do with the way you look or how popular you are with other people. It has nothing to do with your body size, or the things you have accomplished in your life. Self-worth is simply the value you place on who you are as an individual. Do you appreciate yourself as you are now, perceived faults and all?

One of the biggest reasons why you may struggle with your self-worth is the overemphasis on material indicators. When you attach your worth to a career, financial earnings, titles and job prestige, you view your worth in terms of money, success, achievements and possessions – the type of car you have, the neighbourhood you live in, the size of your house, or the title you hold at your place of work all become a way by which you undervalue your worth

When you have a healthy level of self-worth you can acknowledge your strengths and weaknesses. You can feel good about yourself for who you are and while you recognize you are not perfect and have faults.' you don't allow what you are not right now define how you see yourself.

So how can you boost your self-worth? I am a big believer in the fact that you can't fix what you don't know exists. So you need to self-explore and get a health status on your self-worth. You can begin by taking a self-worth inventory; just what do you think about yourself? A self-analysis will help you recognize where you're short-changing yourself.

► Take a notebook and write down your top ten strengths. They can comprise your talents which are innate and your skills which are things you've learned and an expertise you possess. Initially you may think you don't have any, but you do. Think about what other people say to you, even if you don't say it to yourself. "You're so patient", "You're very generous", "You're great fun to be with", "You're kind", "You're a great leader", "You know so much" or "You are really good at your job". Take some time every day to look at your strengths in greater detail. Start thinking about how you can make the most of them in the things you choose to do because they can become even a greater sense of strength for you.

► Now do the exact same exercise but this time write down your top ten weaknesses. It's most likely a lot of these have formed into beliefs about yourself so you will need to work on changing the specific beliefs as outlined in chapter sixteen 'Creating New Beliefs'. Only work on weaknesses that you think limit your life and limit what you're trying to achieve. Your focus should be your strengths, but by understanding what is limiting you, you can boost your strengths.

▶ Ask yourself the following questions: What do I want to be doing with my life? Am I doing it? If not, why not? What makes me feel fulfilled? Am I working on that or am I busy working on other people's fulfilment?

Boosting your self-worth is one thing but nurturing it is just as important. It is important to be aware of how much respect you give to yourself to start with. People often look to others to validate themselves in many aspects causing them to lose their own power and control. How often do you look to your friends or those around you to make you feel good about yourself? In order to improve your self-worth you need to change how you interact with yourself and also other people. If you look into the mirror and say negative things, or tell yourself you are no good at something, you are going against your personal power and becoming a victim to yourself. As a result, you send messages to your unconscious mind to think and behave in a negative way, this then impacts on the way people interact with you. Nurturing your self-worth happens when you believe in yourself, recognize that you are doing the best you know how, even if a few days later you might see a better way. Here are seven ways by which you can help boost and nurture your self-worth every day.

1. Stop talking about yourself in a negative way, don't put yourself down, rubbish yourself in anyway or make light of your talents. Because how you talk about yourself, and how you see yourself, how you perceive yourself, becomes your reality.

2. Avoid negative people who can inflict their distress and negativity upon you because of their low self-worth and their choices in life. Hang out with people who are willing and happy to share their insights and learnings with you in a positive way.

3. Don't blame other people for your self-worth. Take responsibility for your own self-worth because when you place blame outside your own self, it alleviates the need to look within at your own self, to change your behaviour, attitude and beliefs. When you blame situations or other people you give up your own power to change everything in your life.

4. Learn to love yourself as you do your best friend. Treating yourself as you would your best friend and coming to love all that you are, the person you were, are and will be. Loving yourself is not expressed through preening oneself all day and constantly announcing how great you are, as that is actually insecurity. Loving yourself is about treating yourself with the same care, generosity and compassion as you would treat a special friend free from judgement and criticism.

5. Celebrate and recognize that you are equal to everyone, and that your abilities, your thoughts and your emotions are

unique and worthy of being shared and heard by the world around you. Stop comparing yourself with others. Nothing will damage your self-worth more than making comparisons between you and other people. The only person you should be comparing yourself with is you.

6. Grasp the opportunities that come your way. Part of building self-worth is learning to recognize opportunities, however small they may appear initially, and working with them. You may have to demonstrate patience even downsizing of your goals and what you're looking to achieve for now. Take the opportunities that life offers you and make the most of them because nothing is ever as it appears to be. A small opportunity can lead you to bigger ones down the line.

7. Affirmations, positive self-talk and visualization are the fundamental part of not only boosting but also nurturing your self-worth. Your ego is built upon what other people say to you whereas your self-worth is built upon what you say to yourself. Check out chapter sixteen 'Creating New Beliefs' for how to do positive self-talk, affirmations and visualizations. I have provided a comprehensive list of affirmations that you can say to help boost and nourish your self-worth in chapter eighteen 'Affirmations and Declarations'.

Maintain your focus on nourishing and boosting your self-worth as an important part of what you do every day. Make time every day to do the work and declare the affirmations. Be self-aware of what's coming to the surface from the work you are doing. Be patient as it takes time to change how you have been programmed. Stop the negative self-talk and putting yourself last, now. The past has its lessons from which you've learned but it's long gone, so leave it behind you. The only moment that truly matters is now. It is the only moment that 'is', after all. Nothing else is a sure thing. And if this moment isn't what you want to be, you can make a different choice for the next moment. We are all responsible for our self-worth and building it back up to its natural state. Self-esteem and feeling worthy is the gift you give yourself.

" Shift your FOCUS to the things you know and do well. Play to your *strengths*, not your *weaknesses* and be INSPIRED rather than *discouraged.* **"**

—Michael Nulty

CHAPTER SEVENTEEN

Affirmations and Declarations

I have put together some of the most powerful affirmations and declarations that I have used in my life, specifically to boost self-worth and develop self-confidence. It is always important to choose the affirmations which resonate with you the best and change them daily or weekly. You can also create your own affirmations as long as they are said in positive words and in the present tense. You say it as you want it to be, not as it is right now or will be in the future. For example, "I accept myself as I am", "I believe in myself", "I am successful in everything I do". It is not necessary that you believe your affirmations, all you have to do is repeat them for now, the believing comes afterwards.

1. It's easy for me to speak up for myself. I am becoming more confident every day.
2. I take responsibility for myself and I clear all the ways my blame is harming my life.
3. I see only the best in myself and others.
4. I surround myself with kind and loving people who bring out the best in me.
5. I am smart and capable of doing everything I put my mind to.
6. I believe in myself.
7. I recognize the many good qualities I have.
8. I release all negative thoughts and feelings about myself.
9. I always think positively about myself and about my life.
10. I love and accept myself as I am.
11. I am always growing and developing.
12. I am unique and it feels great to be my true self.
13. Life is fun and it feels good being alive and being me.
14. Opportunities exist for me in every aspect of my life.
15. I choose to be happy right now. I love my life.
16. I appreciate everything I have in my life right now.
17. I admire how courageous I am in spite of any fears.
18. I am positive and optimistic in everything I do.
19. Things are always working out for me.
20. I find it easy to make new friends and I attract positive and kind people into my life.

21. I am okay as I am. I am doing the best I can.
22. I trust myself and I trust life.
23. I choose to be proud of myself.
24. I am worthy of receiving great things in my life.
25. My personality exudes confidence.
26. Every day I become more and more at ease in my own skin.
27. I am the architect of my life and I choose what I look and feel like.
28. I have all the qualities needed to be successful in everything I do.
29. I am always calm and peaceful.
30. All is well in my life.

Affirmations can be used for immediate, short-term results as well, when you want to influence and redirect the thoughts that occur in your conscious mind. For example, in a situation where you are feeling stressed, tense or upset, you can repeat an affirmation, such as "I feel calm and relaxed. I feel calm and relaxed. I feel calm and relaxed", for a couple of minutes. Since your conscious mind can only think one thought at a time, you are able to 'fill' your mind with thoughts that are calming.

Repeating any of the affirmations listed, will give your self-worth the boost and nourishment it needs. You are reprogramming your unconscious mind, so remember that every new belief needs time and attention to flourish. Affirmations when practised deliberately and repeatedly reinforce the chemical pathways in your mind, strengthening neural connections. But don't set yourself up to fail by setting the wrong expectations or by expecting immediate results in a couple of days. You need to repeat and focus on each one for at least ten minutes every day, for a few months. Anything less than that and they will not succeed in swamping out what you already believe with what you want to believe now.

Your words are not just empty sounds they have the power to create energy positive and negative. When you say "I can't" the energy of those words cause the universe to work in opposition to you. But when you say "I can" the universe will bring you all you need to do just that. So speak the words that empower you and the words that will help you change your life and make it the way you want it to be. When you verbally affirm your dreams and ambitions you are instantly empowered with a deep sense of reassurance that what you wish for will become your reality.

Although we come into this life as equals, equal to everything and everyone, the circumstance, society and culture we are born into creates a different perception and perspective. We may begin our journey in different houses, with better opportunities, more money, kinder more loving parents, a higher level of intelligence, maybe it's a vibrant personality or good looks. But regardless of our opening circumstance we all have the power to change ourselves, our lives, to be successful, to love and to be loved, and to embrace our diversity. To see our difference as uniqueness and individuality, to not allow

184

our circumstance be defined by who we are but to learn, grow and evolve from it, and take what we were born with and the struggles we are getting beyond to build our happy, meaningful and fulfilling life.

" Don't get frustrated trying to be POSITIVE all the time. Start by being LESS NEGATIVE and see how the change impacts your life positively. **"**

—Michael Nulty

CHAPTER EIGHTEEN

What Happens Next?

It can be quite easy to think and believe when you're going through hard times that the best years are behind you. The only reason you start to think and feel that you've already lived your best days is because you've become accustomed to projecting the hard times of your present experience into your future. But what if it were possible to fully believe that things are going to get better and that your future holds many more days, weeks, months and years that are better than anything you've lived. That's the thought you should hold onto as you begin creating your next better chapter.

Going from thinking some things are impossible to knowing you can make them happen may feel right now like a giant leap forward, but it only happens one thought at a time. You are on a journey, and that journey is only just beginning. So do what you have to do now, in order to get through to the time when you can do what you want to do in the future. Don't wait for the best bits to come along, wishing you could turn back time and change some of the choices you made. Because your companion – time – is ever present, reminding you that this moment is where life happens and life changes, as in the blink of an eye it becomes the past.

Living in the present is the only real way to live that is free of illusion. Don't get lost in regrets, living in the past, repeating past mistakes and holding onto old conditioning and habits that block you from experiencing the present moment. Through greater self-awareness you will learn when you are present and when you are dwelling outside it and this awareness will allow you to restore yourself to the now, and being able to live consciously anytime you want. Only in the now can you create and begin making your life the way you want it to be.

What you think about and focus on, plays a vital role in how you feel about your life. What you believe you need and want in your present reality to feel good, feel better and be happy is beyond what is happening right now. Your job is to get there. If you've been worried about how the future will turn out because things aren't going as you planned, you overcome those thoughts and feelings by creating your future instead of fearing it. In doing so, you regain control over your emotions and thinking. And you stop seeing yourself as a victim of things happening to you and instead start seeing yourself as a deliberate creator of your reality.

Your reality is a contrast between your perception of what you have and what you think you would like: between who you are and who you believe you are not, but would like to be; and between where you are and where you feel you would rather be. The gap between the two sides creates a separation, dependent upon your perspective of where you are in relation to what you want. And when your thoughts, feelings and beliefs are not up to speed with the changes you want to make, it creates resistance, struggle and conditions that bring hardships into your daily life experience. However, as you elevate your awareness and make choices from a fully aware presence, you gain ultimate power and freedom.

When you notice what you really want and how you feel, you start to dissolve old habits and create new possibilities. In the present, you are your truest self and life is at its very best, always. The present moment is your magnet and your compass. The secret of a healthy mind and body is not to mourn for what is past, not to worry about the future or not to anticipate troubles, but to live in the present moment. You can correct any old thinking by releasing yourself from self-imposed limiting beliefs and allow your true potential to shine through.

It is hard to comprehend sometimes that you are a perceiver of reality and that mostly everything you experience each day gets filtered through your beliefs. So, literally the life you want to have and the life you have are only separated by what you have come to know and what you believe. You don't get what you want or indeed deserve in life, but rather what you have come to believe you can have and receive. But nothing will ever change for you until you change how you see what you have and how you think about what you don't have in your present life. You must be able to put your thoughts beyond what is, in order to attract something more, something different and something better into your life. If you are able to believe that something can become a reality for you, it will.

As you begin working on yourself, it will feel that things are getting worse rather than getting better. It's okay if that happens. It's the beginning of the process and the journey. It's untangling old threads and disconnecting from past selves. You need to just go with it as it takes time and effort to learn what you need to learn and unlearn. You may not see changes instantly, but you will see them, so be patient, because impatience is only resistance to learning. It means you want the outcome without the experience. You need to let yourself learn, step by step and it will get easier as you go along, that I promise you.

So, decide what you would like to be possible for you and begin creating a plan for what happens next. Pick some goals that you think will help you move forward but only make deals with yourself that you can keep otherwise you weaken your own willpower to transform your life. Set your expectations that some things won't always go as you planned, but you have great new tools now to help you cope and move through any life event that would have derailed you before. Make the mental changes and take small steps as you move forward in the direction of your next new chapter.

Making your life better and transforming yourself is all about your personal story. The state of your life is created as a result of the stories you have told yourself and continue to tell yourself. They show up in every aspect of your life, your job, your family, your self-worth, the struggles you have with relationships and money. Subtly, and without noticing it you slowly change and become the stories you tell. It's the law of life, the universe and your own mind. The challenge to changing and transforming your current story is getting beyond what is, your now reality. Choosing a new different narrative, deciding when a new chapter begins or an old chapter is repeated again. When you let go of the stories that no longer serve you, and don't work for the new reality you want to make, your perspective changes and life takes on a different meaning. Change your thinking, and you will transform your life.

Each new chapter gives you an opportunity to create something better and different. With every thought you think and every emotion you feel, you create the seeds for new experiences to come into your reality. You are creating the story, you are living right now whether you know it or not and whether you want to or not. Because you and you alone create your reality and how you perceive your life is the key to unlocking everything you need to begin changing it all.

Life may seem really hard right now, but is it because you have been living to certain limitations that have caused you to believe that you can't overcome the obstacles you're going through? It's time to break free of limitations and change your life for the better.

Well, you've made it this far through the book, so you have the commitment required to create the changes you need in your life and I have no doubt you will succeed. It doesn't really matter where you're starting this journey from, or if your motivation right now is coming out of your love for the people in your life and not your own self. What is important is your decision to choose hope and happiness over depression and despair.

Always remember even through the hardest of times, when life feels hopeless and you are at your very lowest that you are stronger than you feel, smarter than you think and more capable than you know and believe you are in that moment. Be patient, trust in your higher power, believe in yourself and you will experience life as it was meant to be for you.

What I know for sure is that there is no right or wrong path, so be easy with yourself as you find a way to begin your new chapter. Feeling better about yourself, your life, spending less and less time wrestling with your daily demons is life changing and when you make change happen with the desire to learn, grow, heal, and feel happier, you change your life, forever.

" KEEP GOING even if you feel everything is going against you, for that is just the time when the tide of hardships turn and things get **BETTER. "**

—Michael Nulty

CHAPTER NINETEEN

Michael's Life Story

As I look back on my life, I can see my journey so clearly; the choices I made to take one path over another. I can see how every experience has given me the life skills I have today. It took a number of harsh lessons, my life falling to pieces, attempted suicides, being penniless and homeless for me to eventually see life differently and awaken to a new way of living. I don't look back with regret although there were times which I would like to have not experienced. But I've taken the time to make peace with, learn from and heal the wounds of my past.

For many years, other people saw my life so very differently to how I saw it. I really had everything, but I couldn't see it because I was looking at it through a different lens. A lens that showed me what was missing not what was present. I spent all of my life trying to feel good enough. I thought that if I had enough money, if I was successful enough that I would feel good enough. But none of my successes and regardless of how much money I earned ever erased my childhood belief of not being enough, so I continued looking for it until I couldn't look any more. It was only then I discovered the secrets to life! It's quite ironic that I had to lose everything to find everything that I wanted.

We all have our own personal and individual story as to why and how we are where we are in our life right now. This is my story of new beginnings, living with and overcoming depression, finding hope in the darkest of places, connecting with my higher self and spirit guide, dealing with diversity, getting beyond my struggles and taking my life back from fear and struggle.

I was born in a little country village in the county of Dublin, Ireland in 1965. I was the second eldest of five children: four boys and one girl. My father, a farmer only knew country life. His parents died quite young, so as the oldest son he inherited his father's farm and carried on the tradition of farming. My mother couldn't have been more different. She came from the City of Dublin from a long line of musicians. But even more different she spent nearly fourteen years of her early life as a nun, before receiving dispensation from the Pope to leave her religious life. Both of my parents were truly dedicated to providing for us as a family, giving all of their children the very best they could.

My early years were harsh even for that time. But as you know nothing better you accept as a child that this is what life is. Although we had electricity, we had no running water. So no indoor plumbing of any sort. The indoor sink was a basin and our toilet was a large bucket with a wooden lid in a little shed outside which got emptied every day. Getting fresh water was one of our daily chores. My brothers and I would take our handmade cart and a large forty litre milk can to the water pump, which was luckily only two hundred metres away from our home. Getting the can to the pump wasn't too hard. But getting it back home full of water with five, six and seven-year-old boys coordinating who pushed and pulled while arguing, normally resulted in the can falling off the cart and water spilling out. One can of water often took us two or three goes. We often laugh about it now but it was serious stuff back then especially when we got punished for taking so long.

My grandmother lived with us for my early childhood and I had the most wonderful relationship with her. She had rheumatoid arthritis so was confined to a wheelchair. I remember always helping her get dressed every morning and being with her constantly. I still remember the day she passed away. I was seven and I can still see my young self sitting in the corner beside our fireplace in the living room not really understanding what was happening but feeling very lost.

It was at that age when I started to become somewhat aware that I was a bit different to other boys in my school. I didn't have words to explain or the intellect to understand what I was sensing. But I felt that I wasn't the same. But more than being different or the same,

I felt that I was wrong and not equal to everyone else. Desperately wanting to fit in and belong I kept it as my secret. I also kept my distance from other kids and didn't really talk a lot in school. Somehow I had worked out in my little head that if people got to know me they would somehow discover that I was different and dislike and reject me.

Not getting involved, isolating myself meant I seldom got picked to play any schoolyard games and when I did play I was always the last person chosen to go on a team. I remember the tremendous feeling of rejection. I internalized it as being unwanted which only added to my already existing feelings of inequality, low self-worth and a dislike for my own self. But I would fight back the tears and show people I didn't care, when really all I wanted to do was to run away and cry.

I'm not sure whether it was because I was a bit of a loner, shy, or that little bit different that I found myself being bullied in the schoolyard nearly every day. Sometimes I fought back, I didn't want to show them that I was hurting or frightened. Other times I would try to ignore them or just run away from the situation. Every day was pretty much the same, a hardship I kept to myself. I became quite good at hiding my feelings, just bottling everything up.

As I entered my early teenage years, secondary (high) school became a living nightmare. The name calling and bullying not only continued but also escalated. Taking days off school, even weeks became a regular habit to try and escape my school life. It caused me tremendous stress and anxiety and was the beginning of my long time affair with depression. But as depression wasn't something that was talked about I got classed as a moody teenager. I had so much frustration, anger and fear built up inside me and so much hatred of myself that it just poured out of me through tremendous tantrums.

If what I was going through on the outside wasn't enough, my hormones were making my life a misery on the inside. The thing I sensed as a younger boy, my secret was finally presenting itself in real feelings. I tried to ignore everything I felt, hoping that my feelings would just disappear. But they just grew stronger and stronger. I couldn't control them, which was frightening. I hated my feelings because they proved I was different and wrong because I was attracted to boys. This was in the late 1970s and from my upbringing the word 'gay' or 'homosexual' didn't really exist, well not in rural Ireland, in the home of a Catholic ex-nun and a farmer. I felt I was the only person like this. I was truly a freak of nature. Everyone else was talking about girls, getting into girl–boy relationships, even our religious studies were about man and woman, not man and man. I knew for definite that I could never tell anyone what I was feeling. It was going to be my burden and something I would have to live with. It was my secret.

I couldn't understand what was happening, why or how to stop it. I wanted so much to be like everyone else, not different and not wrong. I didn't want to feel anything for anybody. But I did. I even fell in love when I was around sixteen with a special person but being unable to process my own sexual orientation and thinking that I was the only person like me in the world, I did what I knew best, wrapped it up, pushed it deep down inside and pretended nothing was happening at all. It's amazing how much hurt a smile and a laugh can camouflage.

Between the ages of thirteen and sixteen I came to the conclusion that feelings hurt. Liking someone, not being able to tell them or have your feelings reciprocated broke my heart. There was no place in my life for feeling. It was in those years that I began building a wall around myself. I would not be hurt by anyone or anything ever again.

But the wall did more than just keep me from getting hurt it also kept people out, beginning a very lonely period in my life. The feelings I had turned into daily thoughts of killing myself. The idea made me feel as though I had an escape route and gave me some sense of control over my life even if it wasn't real. I had had enough of it all, especially school. I felt that it didn't matter if I were gone. Who cared about me anyway?

As I look back now on my time at school and try to think of some enjoyment I might have had during those days, I can't. It truly was a horrific time for me and one that left many scars and many wounds for me to heal later in my life. The only saviour and shining light in my early years was dancing and music. But my real love for it didn't really blossom until my teenage years. It allowed me to escape into a different world. A world where I excelled and became a great champion of Irish Dancing. A world where my secret didn't appear to be important or even matter. I was a very different version of myself. I was confident and self-assured of the great talent I was gifted with. It was my passion and love of dancing that gave me the strength to carry on living through the hardest of times and the most difficult of environments.

I remember a great weight lifted when I finished secondary school. I was eighteen now and my school days were past. I didn't have to face daily ridicule. I think the relief that it was all over allowed me to think about the future for the first time in a positive way. It felt like a new beginning. I took the confidence I had acquired from being a champion dancer and brought it into the rest of my life. I began seeing life with a new perspective.

For the first time my life was different. My life had possibilities and I was making money, working and spending it all at the same time. I had very little emotional attachment or reactions to anything in my life. Really, I remember feeling nothing much of anything, happy or sad. I had built a wall around myself so that nothing or no one could ever hurt me again and it was doing its job pretty well. A friend told me one time that I didn't have a heart, I had a swinging brick. But then they didn't know at the time how my heart had come to be like stone. I was in no way going to say: "I was tormented and bullied throughout my school life, I am deeply depressed, oh, and I'm gay." I had spent many years convincing myself why I needed to keep everything inside, a secret. And it would take something mighty, to reveal what I perceived was my true identify to anyone.

I was building a new life now. I continued outwardly showing the world this strong, invincible persona. An amalgamation of masks, attitudes and beliefs forming my ego self, which I presented to the world. I began building a professional working career, furthering my education, becoming a teacher of Irish Dancing and opening my very first business with my older brother. I was in my twenties and I was making life work for me as best I could with what I knew.

I was naturally competitive as a child and that followed me into my work life. Being good at something was my way of balancing the books. I thought that if I was successful, had fine clothes and lots of money, I would be seen as a somebody, and that being different, un-equal, wouldn't matter. My self-worth became attached to things and my belief at the time from what I had learned was that a great life, a happy life was something that I would have to find outside myself definitely not something within, because there was nothing joyous going on inside my head.

However, although I showed a strong external attitude to the world, inside I was fighting my demons. I still didn't like myself at all and my self-worth was at its lowest. But no one would ever have known it. I was an expert now at hiding who I really was and how I was truly feeling about anything. But my secret, my struggle, the burden I had carried all my life was getting harder to contain. It was more than being gay. It was fear: the fear of people finding out, of being rejected. I tried on many occasions to talk to people about it, but years of suppressing it, believing I was wrong and believing some made up scenario of what might happen was convincing enough to remain silent.

The period of my life that felt as if it was going well seemed to fade and was replaced with more struggle and hard times. Actually nothing in my life was going right any more and after two years of building a new life, career and business, everything started crumbling around me. My business failed and I had to close it, and very quickly I found myself in the darkest of places and severely depressed. I was exhausted, having battled for most of my life. I had no fight left. And I remember vividly sitting in a chair in a hotel feeling lost and so alone. I thought to myself, "I can't do this anymore", "I can't pretend anymore". I couldn't see any way forward and I couldn't face living another day in the emptiness of my depressed mind. So I decided I would take my life. I was twenty-three years of age.

I remember the first night I attempted suicide. I spent weeks stockpiling medications belonging to my parents – blood pressure, arthritis, heart and other tablets. I didn't know what half of them were for, and I didn't really care. Then one night, I went to bed as usual saying goodnight to everyone knowing that I would never see or speak to any of them again. My heart was broken, I was broken. I had nothing left and I wanted to be free of my torment. I got into bed, swallowed every pill and put on my earphones to listen to a piece of music I had chosen. Tears ran down my face as it suddenly dawned on me what I had just done. It was over now. I didn't have to pretend or hide who I was, any more. I could rest and finally be at peace. But it was not the end.

To my shock I awoke the next day. I couldn't believe I was still alive. My thoughts were, "You couldn't even kill yourself". My worry immediately jumped to what damage had I done to my organs and body. I definitely didn't need any other problems.

My first suicide attempt failed but my second wouldn't! And a few days later, I repeated the process. This time I took twice as many tablets as before. I remember being less emotional about what I was doing this time. I just wanted to get it over with. It was like I wasn't there any more. But yet again I woke up and miraculously with no ailments and no side effects. It was as if I had done nothing but gone to sleep.

My survival gave me a new found strength, which I hadn't felt for a long time. I eventually confided in a friend about my sexual orientation. I took an entire day and many hours of talking to say out loud the words: "I am gay." It felt so good just to say it out loud. I felt so much lighter, I hadn't realized how heavy the burden had become. However, after all of that coming out I thought I would feel so much better, but I didn't. Within two days I started to feel down again. Although I had spoken about it, I still didn't accept myself or like who I was. Nor had I spoken about being bullied or my suicide attempts. I had a long road ahead of me if I wanted to take my life back.

I went to counselling, which I must add was under duress.

Although I had spoken to my friend about my sexual orientation I hadn't talked to anyone else about it and I didn't particularly want to at the time. But my friend could see I was struggling so she took it upon herself to intervene, which I was grateful for, eventually.

My first two counselling sessions didn't really go anywhere. He asked me, "Why are you here?" My reply was, "Don't you know?" The conversation went on and on like that because I couldn't say the words "Because I am gay", which was obviously what he wanted me to say. After really getting nowhere with that question, he asked me, "What do you like about yourself?" I could answer that one, it was an easy one for me. I wanted to say, "I hated myself", but I settled on, "Nothing, nothing at all." But I wasn't going to get off that easily and after an hour I eventually added that "I like my feet". As far as I was concerned that's all there was to like about me.

As I attended a few more counselling sessions I became more comfortable talking about what was going on with me. I began to open up and talk about what being gay meant to me. I never got to talking about my suicide attempts or the bullying. But it helped me to see some things differently. I felt I needed a new start. So I packed up my bags and with the little money I had, I went to America to my aunt and first cousins living in New York, Michigan, and California.

It was great to be somewhere very different and so diverse compared with Dublin at the time. But I discovered that although I had travelled thousands of miles to really get away from my past, my past travelled too. A new country, new experiences, all the travelling was distracting. But the old familiar thoughts and feelings were still there. My demons had gone nowhere. I did what I was used to doing, ignore and suppress everything. The fear of being judged, rejected, not liked still ran through my every thought and emotion.

I knew I still had a lot of work to do, but living in America, working, trying different things gave me confidence and allowed me to see things from a different perspective. I returned to Ireland two years later a very different person. I came out to my friends and family, rented my first apartment, got a great new job and began building my life back again.

Because I had such a difficult time coming to terms with my sexuality I wanted to help other people face it. I helped out on various different 'coming out meetings' and call lines. I wanted people going through anything half as horrendous as I had been through to know that they could feel better about it, one day.

Life was definitely looking up. I was asked to do a two-month dance workshop in New Zealand. I jumped at it. And off to the other side of the world I went. The workshop was a great success and shortly after returning I was asked to go back for a second. This time I decided I would stay longer and check life out down under. It was so hard saying goodbye to my family and friends that I cried nearly the whole journey there. But I felt compelled to go. I was searching for something … what, I didn't know.

I fell in love with New Zealand. For the very first time in my life I felt alive. I felt free. No one knew my past, and so I was who I wanted to be at that time. I was so happy and I fell in love. It was in New Zealand that I came upon Louise Hay's book *You Can Heal Your Life*. It was quite strange the way it happened. My friend asked me to go with her to a crystal healing tradeshow, which I declined, but on the morning of the convention she called to pick me up, thinking I had said I would go. So I ended up going. At the time I had no knowledge of crystals or healing from what looked like pretty rocks. As I walked around trying to pass the time while my friend explored, I came upon a little booth selling books. All the books were about energy healing except three books which were by Louise Hay. Not only did I buy the book *You Can Heal Your Life*, but also the workbook and another book called *The Power Is Within You*. To this day I have no idea why I bought them except that I was being led to that moment where I would receive something that would change the direction of my life.

As I outlined in chapter five 'The Power of Mind', my initial readings didn't go smoothly. But after reading the book many times it started to make sense to me. I was also ready to be open to new ways of thinking and I had this feeling within that what I was reading was true and real. I began doing the work, doing all the exercises, the techniques, mirror affirmations, positive self-talk. It was tremendously hard. It was scary looking into my eyes in the mirror. It felt as if I was looking into my soul. I could see the hurt of my past. And for many months, every time I would say the affirmation "I love and accept myself", I could hear a voice in my head saying "No you don't".

But I persevered and did everything I could to help heal myself and my life.

But just as everything was going so well, it all fell apart. The situation just didn't feel right any more. So, I ended my relationship and not only did I lose a boyfriend but my home, too. All the money I had made teaching was now nearly gone and there wasn't a lot of other teaching work available at the time. I had applied for citizenship but that ended with my relationship. It was a hard decision but I decided to go home to Ireland. Looking back on it now, I can see so many other choices, decisions I could have made; would I have ended up at a different point now? Who knows?

I was now thirty years of age and after many years living on the other side of the world I was now at home living with my parents. It definitely felt like I had gone so far forward only to end up at the same place I started. The old familiar negative thoughts came back into my mind and I could feel my mood changing and slipping back into depression. But one morning when I woke up, I suddenly realized I had tools I could use. I knew so much more now about how to make my life better. Sure, it didn't work out in New Zealand but maybe it was never supposed to or maybe I would understand my reason for being there in the first place in years to come. I started doing my affirmations, my visualization and positive self-talk. I knew the Law of Attraction was going to be responding to my dominant vibration so I tried my best on the days when I just didn't feel like being positive, and there were many, to be as neutral as possible. I only wanted good things to come my way, and that was my focus.

Shortly after being back home, I got a job offer and very quickly after that became a branch manager, and within two years I was the operations director for Ireland for the same company. Things were going well; I had an apartment in the city and a fantastic life with lots of friends and lots of money. The success kept coming. I got an opportunity to open a new marketing business and although it was a bit scary opening my own business again, I went for it. It was a great time and I even fell in love. However, Christmas 1998 saw the passing of my father from cancer. It was a difficult time for all of us in my family especially at that time of year. It sort of set the tone for 1999. It was a difficult year on all levels, both personally and professionally. I tried to expand my business but by the year end it went into liquidation. It hit me pretty hard, having to close a second business. I also had to vacate my apartment and move back into my family home while I sorted out other living arrangements. I was now a couple and I had to consider my partner, too.

I couldn't stop myself from falling back into depression. I went through some horrible months and, of course, taking my life was something that was back on the table. But I couldn't put my mother through that or my partner, so I was lost. I couldn't see a way forward or a way back. I remember just sitting on the couch staring through the window into space for hours and hours. This was now the year 2000 and there were different treatments that could help me with my depression, I wasn't just a moody teenager, but someone with a real diagnosable mental illness. But the shame of being in such a predicament and being depressed wouldn't let me ask for help. So I followed the programme wired in my brain that was still running from my childhood and teenage years and bottled it all up inside.

It took six months for me to put myself back together with the love and help of my family, friends and my partner. I learned during that time, that I was a survivor and that after all the highs and lows I still wanted to find my better life. I would start a new chapter, this was my fourth new beginning.

In only a matter of weeks, I found a new job as a sales manager and like previous jobs my hard work and leadership saw me promoted to Head of Sales for one of the largest brands in Ireland and the world at the time: Yellow Pages. I was back on top again, winning awards, receiving huge yearly bonuses and enjoying life again. But the end of 2003 saw a trip to A&E for my mother turn into her death one week later. It was the most surreal time in all our lives as we spent the week shuffling from one hospital to another as they tried to save her life, she was only seventy-four. Her death hit all of us very hard. I remember going back into our family home and feeling this huge sense of emptiness. It was like the life had left the house, it was just bricks and mortar now. And I thought to myself, "I am all alone now".

Although my personal life was in turmoil, my professional life was still going well; I was a well-respected business leader and influencer. And just over a year after my mother passed I was headhunted to become General Manager of another company in a completely different industry. I took the opportunity to challenge myself and develop my leadership skills. I enjoyed great success there for three years until I felt I couldn't do any more. I wanted to be part of something big. So I applied for a job with one of the largest technology companies in the world: Dell. At the time I didn't really know a lot about technology but I knew that I knew people and how to lead them, inspire and motivate them. So I did my mental work, my affirmations and my visualization. I wanted the Law of Attraction to pick up my good vibes and bring them back to me with a great job. And so it did. I was hired into a role as a senior sales manager which I was happy to accept as I knew once I was in there I was only going to be moving up.

Not long after being hired I was offered the role of head of marketing for United Kingdom and Ireland, and travelled extensively throughout Europe. In total, I won eleven awards in sales and marketing for my work there. And I can only say I spent the most wonderful six and a half years with Dell, it was truly an exceptional place to work with the most talented people in the world.

The end of 2014 brought an opportunity to take redundancy. And although it was a very difficult decision to make, I had this feeling within, a knowing that there was something more for me, this wasn't all there was. What it was I didn't know, but I would soon find out.

I took the opportunity to follow a dream both my partner and I had of living in Spain, the same partner that helped me through my depression back in 1999. And so with hope in our hearts, money in our pockets and a headful of ideas we set off to sunny Gran Canaria, a Spanish island off the coast of Africa, where the sun shone all year round. We had holidayed there for many years so it felt like a home away from home and we hoped we could set up a local business together.

But what started as an idyllic beginning ended up my living nightmare. Not only did I open a business and invest my life savings, but I also closed it within one year. The business idea was great, but the location and a tourist market made conditions very tough for our new business venture. It was a commercial decision to close the business before it started creating debt. But emotionally I felt my heart was ripped out. I mentally fell to pieces and very quickly fell into depression, yet again. I had lost everything financially; although I owned a house in Dublin, the bank was looking to foreclose as as I was struggling to pay the mortgage at that time.

I started to lose my identity. Who was I now? I used to be a hugely successful leader in business, but now I was nobody, living in the most horrid of conditions. I knew this was my final chapter. There would be no more new beginnings.

But it was in the darkest of those days, living in a cockroach-infested house and in the midst of my depression that I found something, a connection, a small light, in what felt like a life of darkness. It changed my entire perspective and relationship with life beyond anything I had ever known, or encountered before.

As I've said before I call this time my awakening. A time when I was done with living and ready to bow out of life but, equally filled with a knowing that there was something more, something better beyond where I was at that moment. It was like my spirit cried out to me to take the next step in my journey, letting me know that finally I was ready to become the person I was meant to be.

Writing this book has allowed me to realize that I spent my life trying to be someone better in the hope I would find that something that could make me feel happy inside without having to continually create the right conditions to bring that happiness about. Linking my self-worth to my professional career gave me a feeling of prosperity and affluence but a false sense of worth and once I stripped away my work and the job, I was left feeling empty inside.

One of the greatest lessons I've learned over the past few years and there have been many, is that my happiness is not dependent on anything or anyone. That happy is something I can become, just like sad and then depressed was something I became. It appears quite logical now but my beliefs about happiness were that it was outside me, in that it was in what I did, who I was, where I lived, how much money I had and what designer labels I wore. It was something I learned and came to believe from my early life – happiness had to be constructed in the physical world for me to feel it in my mental world.

During my earlier years, unknowingly I developed a strong limiting belief that convinced me every day for years that if I could make conditions a certain way and keep them that way my life and my capacity to feel good and be happy would dramatically change. And although money, love, good health, a successful career, loving family and friends did definitely make me feel better and bring great happiness into my life, it always felt temporary because it was conditional living and not living unconditionally.

In getting beyond my struggles, I found unconditional, authentic happiness and so much more. I've moved from a place of great darkness to a life of possibilities and light. The depression that came to visit me has gone and I know that I now finally have all the tools I could ever need to deal with it if it ever returned. Today, I find happiness and contentment in some of the most simplistic things and from just being connected to my spirit self. Although I am planning now for a great future at the age of fifty-two, I live my life one day at a time and one decision at a time. I am excited to see where this new chapter leads me. My life is only just beginning.

" Don't wait until everything is *just right* to change your life. There will *always* be obstacles and less than perfect conditions. JUST START. "

—Michael Nulty

Also by Michael Nulty

LifeTips - Vitamins For The Mind

Check out Michael's next book *LifeTips - Vitamins For The Mind*, and let him continue to help bring light and hope into your life.

Do you know that inspirational quotes have an amazing ability to motivate and change the way you feel about your life right now? They can give you an almost instant pick-me-up on reading them, making you feel happier and more inspired to take action towards what you want in your life.

Vitamins are an essential part of our wellbeing and just as we can take a vitamin supplement to aid a vitamin deficiency in our body, we can use positive and uplifting words as an important ingredient of making our mental life better.

The way you think and feel about yourself, including your beliefs and expectations about what is possible for you, determines everything that happens to you. When you change the quality of your thinking, you change the quality of your life. Just as funny jokes can make someone laugh, positive words can shift your mindset from a negative to a positive, retuning your mind and thinking by reading the right quotes on a daily basis.

LifeTips - Vitamins For The Mind is more than a book of Michael's life tips and inspirational quotes. It also includes inspiring quotes and life tips from ordinary people who have faced failure and success and who despite certain odds and challenges remained positive to take their lives back.

"Be mindful of the words you say about who you are and what you can do. The more often you hear a message – positive or negative – the more you will believe it." Michael Nulty

" Tough times might stick around for awhile, but *they don't last forever.* If you are down right now know you CAN make your life better. "

—Michael Nulty

Connect with Michael

Twitter: @michaelnultyaut
Instagram:@michaelnultyauthor
Facebook:@MichaelNultyAuthor
Linkedin:Michael Nulty
www.gettingbeyondwhatis.com
www.michaelnultyauthor.com

Printed in Poland
by Amazon Fulfillment
Poland Sp. z o.o., Wrocław